The

SECRET

of

PERFECT LIVING

The

SECRET

of

PERFECT LIVING

James T. Mangan

Prentice-Hall, Inc.
Englewood Cliffs, N. J.

LIBRARY OF CONGRESS
CATALOG CARD NUMBER: 63-16356

Reward Edition . . . . . May, 1975

Second Printing . . . . . May, 1976

PRINTED IN THE UNITED STATES OF AMERICA
B&P

To My Daughter

Ruth

*The Pleasantest Person
You Could Ever Hope to Meet*

WHAT IS
THE "SECRET"
OF PERFECT LIVING?

___

More THAN FORTY-FIVE YEARS OF INTENSIVE STUDY AND thousands of experiments with people from all walks of life have gone into the creation of what I call *Perfect Living*. And what is *Perfect Living*?

Perfect Living is a state of absolute self-togetherness, a union of the conscious and subconscious selves for the ultimate good and benefit of your whole person. Though this union of an individual's two selves has been much written and talked about, little has been accomplished to bring it down to a tangible level. In my own mind-science studies I concentrated on discovering a practical method of uniting the conscious mind and the subconscious, and found a technique through which such a union can be achieved.

My technique calls for four easily adopted attitudes and the use of *switchwords*, a means by which the conscious mind can "talk to" and direct the thought patterns of the subconscious. Through these switchwords the conscious person gains the cooperation of his subconscious self, creating an inner harmony that brings immediate results.

For example, how often is your day spoiled by a persistent, nagging pain or headache? Aspirin may bring temporary relief, but it doesn't get to the cause, and the pain returns. Wouldn't it be wonderful to be able to utter a single word which would instantly cause all pain to vanish? There is such a word, and Chapter 9 of this book explains in detail how you can make it work for you.

Or have you ever lost or misplaced some important or valuable possessions? The more desperately you search for the object, the more it seems to elude you. But with one of the magic switchwords you relax and let your Inner Self bring you to the thing you are searching for. Chapter 8 covers the details on how you can turn on your own finder machinery.

These are only two small examples of what *Perfect Living* and its switchwords can do for you. With *Perfect Living* you can do anything. You can:

1. Conquer all your fears.
2. Learn to relax.
3. Keep yourself forever young.
4. Overcome despair and "blue" moods.
5. Begin to know yourself.
6. Get along better with other people.
7. Set goals and achieve them.
8. Gain money and new prosperity.
9. Free yourself of bad habits.
10. Achieve glowing health and freedom from pain.
11. Release your hidden abilities.
12. Be a permanently happy person, invulnerable to any upset or setback.

But the benefits of *Perfect Living* are endless and the book itself explains them all to you. Why not put this modern miracle to work now? Make *Perfect Living* a part of your life!

CONTENTS

6

Submission to the Higher Power (*Continued*)

Skip Your Morning Bath (53), The Many Varieties of Submission (53), The Sweetness of Convalescence (53), Over the Hill to Oneness (54), PRACTICES IN SUBMISSION (54): Call the Feeling by Its Most Shocking Name (55), Artificial Elation (55), Produce Something, Do Something (58), The Bricklayer Gazes Proudly at His Wall (58), Good Work Is a Lot of Fun (59), Walk Fifty Feet Thinking of Every Step You Take (59), REMINDER (60), "Fanatics Not Wanted" (60), An Emerson Paradox (61), Lack of Conscious Direction Can Mean Sudden Death (63), All Excesses Need Help From the Conscious (63), Invite the Conscious In (64).

7

Testing the Words of Power (65)

TRY THE SWITCHES! (66), A Mild Relaxer (66), To Stand Up Straight (67), He Switched on Instant Politeness (67), It Is Real Fun to Be Polite (68), To Prolong a Fine Feeling (68), Familiar Actions Can Be Switches (69), Help Yourself to Generous Snacks of Perfect Living (69), "Together" Has Magic (70), "Together" Helps Him Sell (70).

8

How to Find Lost Treasures (72)

You Know and You Don't Know (73), "Don't Stop Now, Keep Going" (73), BETTER Than Reason or Common Sense (74), You Against Yourself (75), Mistakes in Living (75), This Machine Easy to Test (76), Solving Problems While Asleep (78), Finding the Key That "Unlocks" the Buyer (79).

18

How to Satisfy Your Every Desire (156)

19

A Key for Every Lock (166)

20

The Mind-Machines in Action (174)

21

The Magic Power of Wanting (188)

21

The Magic Power of Wanting (*Continued*)

(191), Private Telepathic Machines? (192), Cases of Act, Fact, Symbol (193), Reports on "Be" for Form (194), Avoid "Imperfect Living" (194), "Care" Is a Fine Switchword for Sensational Feats of Memory (195), For Fingernail Biters (197), "ALWAYS A FIRST TIME" (198), Case of the Wandering Topcoat (198), How Three People Helped Themselves (201), How Three People Fall Asleep (202), The Power of Want (203).

22

You Are Not Alone (205)

Ways to Develop and Expand the Pro-Conscious (206), Say a Silent "Thank You" (206), Their Antennae Work for Them (206), Establishing Personal Perspective (208), A New Slant on Self-Discipline (209), Tips for Balancing the Psyche (209), Reading Yourself Out Loud (210), Sympathy From the Sub-Soul (212), Let Your Pro-Conscious Tell You What to Do (213).

23

The Great Joy of Perfect Living (216)

First Proposition (216), Second Proposition (217), Third Proposition (217), Fourth Proposition (218), Fifth Proposition (219), Sixth Proposition (219), SEEK YOUR FIRST GOAL FIRST (220), The Hints of Something Bigger (220), No Answer in the "Little Things" (220), Apartness Vanishes When Submission is Invoked (221), The System at Work (221), Prompt Encouragement (222).

1

A NEW
PUSH-BUTTON SCIENCE

Are THERE SOME DAYS WHEN EVERYTHING YOU DO SEEMS to go wrong? On these occasions, don't you feel that there are two sides of your nature fighting it out with one another? One side seems to try its best to thwart everything the other attempts. Take the story of the shoe clerk, for example.

The Shoe Clerk Quoted Goethe

The shoe clerk was making headway. All he needed to do was to get the second shoe on the other foot, prove it was as comfortable as the first and the sale was in the bag. But at the critical moment, he couldn't find his shoe horn. "Where could I have put it?" he asked in mild panic; "I just had it in my hands." He began to shove sundry objects around frantically.

But his customer was cool and patient. In a calm voice the customer said, "We do these things to ourselves." The clerk turned suddenly and laughed. "How true, how true!" he exclaimed, "and Goethe, the great German poet, said it even better."

He quoted Goethe: "There are two souls in my own breast, and one is determined to beat down the other." One of these souls, with the cunning of a mother fox, the skill of a professional card sharp, had managed to hide the shoe horn right under his nose.

Yes, we do do the darndest things to ourselves. But once in a long while we hit a day when everything goes just right. We get a lot of lucky breaks. We produce fast and neatly. Nothing seems to bother or disturb us. We feel that the fight inside has subsided. We feel great. We *are* great!

The Battle of the Drapes

At least seven times out of ten you pull the wrong cord, although, mathematically, the odds dictate that constant use must cause you to pull the correct cord most often when you want to open or close the drapes.

When you do pull the wrong cord, however, something seems to say: "Listen, wise guy, I made you make this mistake just to show you aren't so smart after all." The feeling comes that one side of you, the trouble-making side, has a better memory, a more cunning brain, and more devilish gifts, than your conscious side.

Gone Yet Near

We mislay or misplace dozens of objects every day and waste precious minutes trying to find them. Usually they are only a few feet away, hidden from our eyes and hands.

Old Bill, friendly and talkative, has suddenly lost his desire to chat with fellow guests in the hotel where he has lived for thirty years. And for a good reason. All at once, he finds himself unable to remember most of their names. Bill is sad, and what has happened to him could be a fatal catastrophe. But there is still hope. All of us, young or middle-aged, do have streaks when suddenly the names of familiar friends and old companions seem lost. If we fight hard to think of the name quickly, it becomes more fugitive and embarrassing. We *know we know* the needed name but cannot *announce* it with our lips.

The shoe clerk knew he knew where the shoe horn was but could not say so out loud. The housewife looking for the scissors, the husband looking for the case for his glasses, *does know* where the missing article is, but something of his own making, *of his very self*, prevents the knowledge from coming into the open.

Every desire and distress is attended by similar roadblocks to peace of heart. The story of every human life might well be: "Two Souls at War Inside Same Person."

A New Push-Button Science

One day I was riding in a cab from Idlewild Airport in New York to the center of town. Because most New York cab drivers are so keen and sophisticated in conversation, I decided to tell my driver a little about the new push-button science of Perfect Living.

No old-fashioned work was required. The two souls Goethe described should get together. But they don't want to get together. They want to fight. The stronger and bigger of the two, often called the subconscious, but really much more than the subconscious, is the one with nearly all the experience.

But the little and weaker soul, which we know as the conscious mind, is the boss of the person and like a silly little office boy is eternally giving orders to the big underself, the real president of the corporation. The president then goes out to fight down the little office boy and it knows how. This is why the two souls seldom are together. But they ought to be together all the time and if they were, life would be heavenly, living would be Perfect.

The Theory of the Switches

I told him about the theory of the switches—the one-word switches which could set mighty and personal machines to work if want and belief were present. His machinery of experience—everything he had ever done, or imagined, or dreamed, or felt in even the smallest twinge of instinct, was likened to any immense line-up of versatile automatic machines ready to deliver any desire or eliminate any distress almost at will.

The one-word favorite slogan of Tom Watson, father of the International Business Machine Computers, was *Think*. Different wants and different distresses call for other one-word switches to turn on the computing machinery inside every human being. Of course, he asked for examples. I could recall many off hand.

Many Examples

A case in point had happened just a week before in Chicago. A young salesman, a student of push-button living, was going to the barber shop early to get the first choice of barbers. Approaching his car, the key ring that held his car keys broke open, and one key—to the door of the garage—fell out.

He distinctly heard it tinkle as it hit the cement floor but looking for it hurriedly, could not find it. He pulled his car out of the garage and looked again. He was sure it hit the floor, because he had heard it hit the floor and, quickly examining the cuff of each trouser leg, he knew it was not there.

"I have to get to the barber," he said. "I will make a thorough search for it when I come back; it is surely somewhere on this garage floor."

The Lost Key Came Back

Parking his car near the barber shop, he began to meditate on the lost key and the strangeness of its disappearance. It would be a big inconvenience not to be able to find it again. He wondered if he should invoke Perfect Living, say "Reach," and see what would happen. He did. Immediately he heard the familiar tinkle on *this* cement sidewalk. Looking down, there was his garage key on the sidewalk, the very same key he had lost two minutes before in his own garage a quarter of a mile away!

"No, no," said the cab driver, enthralled but unbelieving, "such a thing could never have happened."

"But it did," he was told; "this young man had searched the trouser cuff of his right leg thoroughly, and had given only a passing inspection to the left leg cuff, being SURE the key was somewhere on the floor. The only explanation possible was that it was in the left cuff, and when he said 'Reach' in front of the barber shop his left leg gave a slight, automatic, but unconscious kick, and threw the key out on the sidewalk. And if the young man hadn't been alert enough to hear the second tinkle, the key would have been lost forever."

Beat an Eye Operation by Two Months

There was the case of the forty-year-old man who began to be troubled with chalazions, sometimes called "Hailstones," little hard growths on the eye lid, not dormant like a cyst and not nearly as quick to come to a head as a sty. The eye specialist told this man that one of these growths could not be touched with a knife for two months. This was trouble. For the eye lid was beginning to droop with the weight of the chalazion and was very annoying.

A friend who had heard of the push-button theory gave this man the magic switchword. He said. "Just say 'Change,' then let yourself go limp and proceed to do automatically whatever your instincts suggest."

Following instructions, the man went down to his basement, and as if walking in his sleep, picked up a tennis racket and ball, and proceeded to volley the ball against the basement wall. Focusing was required in the little game, and enjoying the new skill he was acquiring, the man practiced the volleying for three days. The chalazion was soon healed.

Regained Fifty Pounds Automatically

Seventy-year-old Jim B. dropped in weight from 180 to 130 pounds and might have gone down to nothing, had not a friend suggested he use the same switchword, "Change." He did not operate this switch in an orthodox manner, but what he did do was *change doctors*. New prescriptions and medicine brought him back to 180 pounds, and he is healthier now than he has been in many years.

Beat the Plumber Out of Ten Dollars

A young sales promotion man, living in the suburbs, where water is expensive, found his water closet was leaking noisily day and night. He tried his best to stop the leak, but not being "mechanical," failed. It worried him and his wife for days. Each inspection of the inside of the top chamber disclosed an arrangement of complicated and mystifying components. He did not want to call a plumber, who would charge at least ten dollars for a call. So he consulted a friend who he thought had mechanical prowess. The friend told him: "You're just as mechanical as I am. The switchword for solving a problem is 'Reach'; tell yourself you want that toilet fixed, and let yourself go automatic."

This suburbanite was willing to try anything to beat the plumber out of ten dollars. So he said, "Reach," automatically walked toward the water closet, picked up a screw driver, lifted the lid, saw a small screw at the top of a pipe, screwed it down a few turns and the leak stopped for good.

Made $20,000 Extra in One Year

One skeptic, ambitious and worldly wise, told a friend Perfect Living was a lot of hooey. Asked what he most wanted out of life, he replied, "Money, of course." He was told the switchword for delivering money was "Find," and that if he could solemnly confirm the personal resolution and begin a serious campaign to make $10,000 extra in the next year, he would reach his goal. All he needed to do was use the switchword "Find" frequently, and keep the "$10,000 extra" objective constantly in mind. The skeptic, thinking, "What can I lose?" tried the switch, let his buried machines of experience come into play, and that next year made $20,000 more than his regular income.

You Can Do Anything

Briefly the driver would interrupt to ask me a few respectful questions. The gist of each query centered around: "How can it be? How can it be? How can life be so automatic?" I would answer: "Anybody can do anything because *he has already done everything* in fact, in imagination, in dream, in unconscious, or surreal life."

Take subliminal advertising in the movie theatre. They flash an ad on the screen so fast you cannot see it or read it. But still you get the message and go out to buy popcorn or a soft drink. Who can explain how a person bends his fingers? Or digests food? What triggers laughter in the human being, a wholly automatic, spontaneous outburst?

Laughter Has to Be Automatic

You can smile on purpose but you cannot command yourself into a genuine laugh—it has to be automatic. I used the illustration of the device for yawning. "Rest the tip of your tongue against the back of your lower front teeth. Now proceed to yawn artificially. You can go through the motions of a yawn, but the artificial yawn is not quite as relaxing as an automatic yawn. However, keep touching the back of your lower front teeth with your tongue, force an artificial yawn, then forget all about the test. In a minute or two you will be automatically yawning your head off." He was and I called it to his attention.

Laughing, he asked, "How can I get hold of all the switch-words I need for this new system?" I was about to tell him that he would have to wait for this book to be written; in the meantime he might use the master switch to his whole subterranean factory of experience, *TOGETHER*. Just then we had to stop at a stop light.

Free as Time and Fresh Air

Another cab pulled up alongside us and its driver, through his open window shouted, "What are you two guys talking up?" I shouted back: "Perfect Living." He then addressed himself to my driver: "Listen, Mac," he said, "is it all right if I park my car right here and get into your cab with the two of you?" "Not on your life," replied my driver, and pulled away as the light changed.

I guessed he reasoned a good thing was a good thing and not to be shared indiscriminately. But I made no protest, for Perfect Living, once understood, is as free as time and as handy as fresh air. All mankind can share in it to the hilt. And I feel that the second cab driver has been by now paid back for his genuine compliment to me. As sure as you sit there, he is owning this book on Perfect Living right now.

2

THE
TWELVE
ANSWERS TO LIFE

About EIGHTY BILLION PEOPLE HAVE LIVED SINCE THE world began, but who has found out how to live perfectly? Some men call life a blessing; others consider it a trial. If there is joy in life, how do we get it? Misery certainly exists in life; is there a way to reduce it or eliminate it entirely?

Every man eventually asks himself the overpowering question:

"What do I most want out of life?"

Throughout the ages scholars and seers have sought the secret of Perfect Living. Aristotle contended: "It is better to philosophize than make money." But Herodotus countered: "Never cut yourself off from your base of supplies."

The Seven Sages of Greece believed all men could find peace of heart in these precepts:

Know Thyself
Avoid Excess
Know Thine Opportunity
Self-Confidence Goes Before All
The Greatest Blessing Is the Power to Do Good

Touchstones for the elite life have been offered by other elite brains:

Common Sense—*Socrates*
The Greatness of God—*Plato*
Bear and Abstain—*Epictetus*
Appreciate the Ideal—*Augustine*
All True Things Square—*Thomas Aquinas*
Observe Nature—*Francis Bacon*
Only One Substance—*Spinoza*
I Think, Therefore I Am—*Descartes*
Sympathy Is the Rule of Morality—*Adam Smith*
Pre-Established Harmony—*Leibnitz*
General Law—*Kant*
Infinite Activity—*Hegel*
We Ought to Be Miserable—*Schopenhauer*
Experience the Source of Certainty—*John Stuart Mill*
Moral Intuition—*Herbert Spencer*
Survival of the Fittest—*Charles Darwin*
Think Straight—*Bertrand Russell*
Life Is Better Than Logic—*Santayana*
Judge Truth by Results—*William James*
The Good Man Is He Who Is Growing Better—*John Dewey*
Education Makes Happiness—*Robert Hutchins*

These are all noble principles, but none or all, in themselves, contain a complete foolproof system for living a life.

If, in your imagination, you interview the eighty billion people who lived in earth's recorded history, and ask each individual what he most wants out of life, instead of getting billions or millions of answers, you will get just about *twelve*—not many more —basic answers. Twelve out of eighty billion possible! And the particular goal in life that you have set for yourself, the objective which up till now you thought you most wanted to reach, is to be found in these twelve:

1. GOD

The acceptance of God as your ultimate end; union and communion with Him, now and through eternity. The code which says that the goodness or badness of your individual acts is determined by how they aid you or retard you from attaining this ultimate goal.

2. SERVICE TO FELLOW MAN

It is better to give than to receive. Love your neighbor as yourself. Serve your fellow man as you would your blood brother, for all men are truly brothers. This was Christ's teaching, a glorious gospel that has carried many followers to heights of personal ecstasy.

3. WISDOM

The goal of wisdom offers the great prize of personal peace— peace of mind and peace of conscience. This school of living need not depend on religion; it gets all its ingredients from Nature and Nature's laws. It urges man to withdraw from worldly strife and struggle, stop trying to get ahead of others and to find contentment in himself alone. He should look at life as if it were a movie on a screen, separate and distinct from him, the viewer.

4. THE LIFE OF ACTION

We all find ourselves thrust into this life, willy-nilly. We are forced to do things, to work, to make, to build, to produce, to reproduce. Success is our target, passion and energy our chief means of making a bull's-eye.

5. ART

The real art spirit is the basic drive to be GREAT, SUPERB, MAGNIFICENT. The true artist, in the rigors of his self-discipline, copies the saint; in his hour of glory he resembles the angel. But the life is too difficult, too lacking in financial reward. We excuse ourselves by granting: "Art is for the few, not the many."

6. SECURITY

This is the system that emphasizes *safety first*. Your life is in constant danger—save it. Never worry about HOW you live; only be sure to live as long as you can. Protect your future by saving your money, and ward off the terrors of dependency in your old age. Because FEAR is everyone's great personal enemy, this school of living is respected by all without contest.

7. HAPPINESS

Every man says: "I want to be happy!" But too few work for happiness seriously, fight for it as they should for a prize so dear. Happiness remains a purely academic thought. It is really the dream result of many other means and ends, of preliminary goals whose realization produces happiness. The brief interludes of happiness we all feel convince us that happiness is desirable, but we would dearly love to know *how to be happy all the time!*

8. MONEY

For most of us the goal of money epitomizes happiness. The sage says: "Money does not necessarily bring happiness," but the universal reply is: "Give me a million dollars and I'll show you you're wrong!"

The great allure of money is that *its idea is simple*. It is a measurable, detectable commodity, in which is packaged, we suppose, most of our wants and needs. It buys things. It keeps us alive. If we had more we could get more out of life.

Money as a goal fits in nicely with life in the world of action into which we are thrust. Few of us garner a great deal of money in a whole lifetime; but we wish for it fiercely, strive for it valiantly.

9. PLEASURE

"Eat, drink and be merry for tomorrow you may die." The voluptuary and sensualist insist life is just a bowl of cherries, not to be taken seriously. The best way to conquer life is to see how much fun you can get out of it.

Pleasure, it seems, should be the first page in the book of happiness. But society says: "A little legitimate pleasure is all that the law allows." Millions resort to sports and entertainment to find surface joy and temporary distraction. They are far from being pleasure maniacs, but they try to give most of their spare hours to entertainment and relaxation.

10. HEALTH

The sick and the old acclaim health as the greatest thing in life, and insist: "You never know how much health means till you lose it."

The specter of pain hangs over us all. Pain is so powerful that, indirectly, it may be considered an instrument of happiness, for when pain stops, the resulting relief is an acceptable substitute for real happiness. Judged coldly, health cannot be said to be a true goal in life or even a worthy goal. For he who puts health above all else is merely saying: "My principal aim in life is to be a good vegetable!"

11. LOVE

More than one poet and philosopher has said: "Love is the greatest thing in the world." Personal love, love of family, love of country, love of nature. We will grant there is not enough love in the world. We will hurry to concede, too, that there could be immeasurably more love, if we would only open the flood gates of our hearts, and let the love out.

The heart fountainhead is inexhaustible. But the cheapness and stinginess of man prevents him from loving to anywhere near his capacity. If self-love reigns supreme, pure love has small chance of coming to flower. Hence, whoever strives to live the life of love, does so in sudden spurts and stops.

12. SELF-DEVELOPMENT

"You can be better than you are," says the inspirationalist. "Every day in every way I am getting better and better," says the auto-suggestionist. Hardly anyone takes exception. The voice of conscience keeps repeating endlessly: "Improve! Improve!" No man should ever be satisfied with his lot—his job, his ability, his education. Often his drive to raise his status catapults him towards the goals of fame and power, bigger objectives still, but destinations freighted with danger of self-destruction.

In pure and simple self-development he has a system of living that enlarges as it unfolds. The acquisition of each new strength and skill carries with it a self-satisfaction few other systems can deliver. As you develop your mind, you can almost *see* this burgeoning of self, a divine fulfillment of your basic instincts for growth and virtue.

All the Answers Are Confusing

Each of the eighty billion humans in history had a different set of fingerprints. The varieties of their nerves, emotions and instincts could never be catalogued. No two of them ever looked exactly alike in face or body structure.

Yet approximately twelve basic wants in life were enough of a choice for all. Several of these basic schools of living are opposed to one another. The man who wants God and the man who wants excessive pleasures are totally opposite. The wise life of contemplation is directly opposed to the driving force of the life of action. So the twelve theses for living have resulted in confusion. We all follow one or more of the goals as we struggle to live, but in the struggle we are always aware that the scheme or schemes we are following are imperfect.

3

HEAVEN

ON EARTH

All MEN DESIRE HAPPINESS. THEY DO NOT KNOW EXACTLY what is meant by happiness, but they desire it just the same.

And all of us, at some time or another have, for all too brief a moment, experienced the feeling commonly called "heaven on earth."

You may have had a good sleep the night before. After a satisfying breakfast, you walk out into the street and find a beautiful sunny day. The world is lovely and life is beautiful. Trouble has vanished. You have not a care or worry in your heart.

Or you have received good news. You have suddenly made money, good fortune has touched you. Or you have finished a difficult task and know you have done it well. And you have been worthily praised for an accomplishment you are sure is praiseworthy.

Such heavenly feeling is the best proof of happiness realizable, because you are right now realizing it. All men feel it at some time, some more than others. We all know that at some time in our own lives we have had it, and it was good, oh so good. If we could only feel this way forever, life would indeed be perfect.

The Nature of the Perfect Living Feeling

Recall the last time you felt this way, or examine yourself the next time you are in the throes of the Perfect Living feeling, and you will agree that the outstanding characteristic of the feeling is this: You are at peace with the world and with *yourself*. Nothing bothers you in that glorious moment, neither people, nor the world, nor *yourself*.

The internal artillery stops firing. You have no fault to find with your own life or with life in general. The war between your conscious mind and your subconscious, subsurface personality is over. This poisonous, deadly, peace-destroying war, has suddenly ceased. You are no longer two separate individuals, two enemy sides, fighting each other with all your might.

One Person Instead of Two

Your "you," the conscious mind, is no longer a separate and distinct entity from "yourself," the subconscious and subsurface you. You feel like a million dollars. This rare feeling, which infrequently touches nearly all of us, can best be identified as the state of having the two sides of self together. In such a golden moment your two souls, the two sides of you, see eye to eye, feel heart to heart, and make you one person instead of two.

Your conscious knowledge is what you know, what you can put into words. Your subconscious knowledge is almost infinite in scope, because, as we use the term in this book we want it to mean every bit of unconscious, subconscious, surreal, subliminal, automatic experience you have ever had.

Only an infinitesimal part of this experience can be remembered in the sense that you can recite it out loud. Nor can you recognize it by sight. It is very much like the huge iceberg, a tiny part showing above water but the immense bulk of it under the surface, invisible, undetectable, but extremely powerful and dangerous.

Also Like a Modern Automatic Computer

Again this same subconscious can be likened to the automatic computer of the modern electronic business machine. It feeds back its own experience on itself. It stores up and multiplies all personal experience—the experience of fact, thought and feeling, as well as the experience of dream, imagery, surrealism or mind mystery.

Because of ignorance, lack of desire to get closer to our subconscious selves, we magnify the importance of the conscious mind. It speaks, and it speaks out loud, for the whole of the personality, because the subconscious has no speaking power of its own.

Thus the conscious continually slurs and insults the subconscious, minifying its importance, often denying its very existence, and this starts the internal war all over again.

The War Is On

The conscious wants the person to do one thing because logic, straight thinking and convention say it is the right thing. The subconscious, perversely, prefers the very opposite. Because it is so big, so experienced and so powerful, it resists being bossed by the "insignificant" conscious mind. The war is on.

Seldom does the conscious get its way. For one person who stays on a reducing diet, or any abstinence program, a hundred others fall by the wayside. The hidden self, balking, cajoling, tempting, and double-crossing, turns the attempted reform into dismal failure.

For the diet was a conscious decision. It represented a good goal commanded by reason and sound arguments. It should be done, but the rebellious subconscious is not interested in what should be done; it resents any command or strong-arming by the conscious. After all, it is the biggest part of you and should have a lot to say. Even when you think you have overcome it, conquered it, and managed to stay on the strict reducing diet for months, it may slyly and diabolically turn the diet into a fiasco by leading you to starve yourself into dire illness, while still thinking your conscious mind is calling the shots.

One Want Instead of Twelve

Instead of there being only twelve or more different kinds of life or wants representing life goals, there should be only one immediate want and all mankind will be served to its complete satisfaction if this first want can be achieved. Because in his realization of this proper first want, man then can easily go on to any further goal in life.

This first want should be the first and only immediate goal of the man of God as well as of his opposite, the man of Pleasure. Likewise this single want is the right immediate goal which makes the artist a complete artist, which makes the sick man well, the frightened man brave, the poor man rich, the failure successful.

Shown this simple key to Perfect Living we should all say: "We no longer need twelve different answers to the challenge of life; this single thesis is enough for us all."

The new thesis can be put into a short sentence. To achieve the ultimate in personal joy, to find perpetual, uninterrupted heaven on earth, all you have to do is:

> *Get your conscious and subconscious selves together and hold them together for every second of your entire life.*

4

HOW

TO FIND

THE SECRET SIGN

For MORE THAN FORTY YEARS THE AUTHOR HAS BEEN trying to find the key to Perfect Living, reading the great books, studying the great philosophers, engaging in voluminous research and experiment.

A Forty-Year Search

As the decades flew by, I investigated one new theory after another; delved deeply into thought transference, psychokinesis and other phases of parapsychology; worked and counseled as an amateur psychiatrist; probed the mystic depths of religion; wandered in the labyrinthine recesses of surrealism and the surreal life; swam in the deep waters of design; and studied intimately the progress of the automationists.

Early in 1951 a stirring inside seemed to presage a great new discovery. I had just finished a year-long study of space and its nature and from that study advanced into an investigation of the speed of light and an attempt to find a speed faster. Of a sudden, all the things I had ever worked on, all the subjects I had ever studied, seemed to merge into one big steaming stew, while my mind kept on echoing a crude thesis of my earlier years: *"There's a one-word formula for everything!"*

At the instant of noon, Sunday, March 10, 1951, a word fell out of the sky and into my arms. I hugged it to my bosom and embraced it as a *sign*, a breakthrough from the divine realm, a super-inspiration. The word seemed to be alive and, like a living spirit, it said confidently and unmistakably, "I am the HOW in 'How to achieve happiness on this earth.'"

The Perfect Formula for Living a Life

The magical, heaven-sent word that came to me that day brought with it the perfect formula for living a life, the revelation of the first and immediate aim in the life of every man.

The word was the familiar, supremely obvious word: "TO-GETHER."

I began saying *Together* to myself quietly, easily, without command. No exclamation point followed it, and no verb or adjective was connected with it. *Together*. Nothing else. *Together*. Then a pause. Then—*Together*.

Touched Off a Deep Contented Sigh

Every time I said the word to myself, a remarkable reaction took place. The word would touch off a deep, prolonged sigh of a quality I had not known for years. Now a sigh is a natural body reflex; something makes you sigh. You do not sense it coming on, you are in the middle of it before you know it, and then there it is.

Every deep natural sigh is a nice thing. It brings relief from some inward tension. It is notification that minor turmoil is subsiding or evaporating.

Each time I said *Together* a grand sigh followed; I could feel gushes of tensions, ancient and recent, being released. So I repeated the magic word over and over and kept on sighing and feeling better by the second.

The Happiest Week

There followed what was for me the happiest week I have ever lived. It had its normal share of setbacks and disappointments, but all negative factors were powerless to scratch the surface of my new harmony. For after a half century of fighting with myself, wrestling with myself on every little problem and decision, I suddenly found myself *on my own side*.

I could find nothing wrong with anything that happened; no fault with any person I met, or knew, or thought of; no temptation to criticize people or events; no intolerance of stupidity or prejudice. All fear had left me, especially the fear of being hurt by anything coming from the world outside me. Everything pleased; nothing bothered. To keep my tank of joy constantly overflowing, all I had to do was say a silent *Together*. A delicious sigh would follow and a delicious oneness pervade me.

Was It a Dream or an Illusion?

Feeling that such heavenly intoxication might not be legitimate, I asked myself: "Is this a dream, an illusion, a sign of mental disbalance?"

I decided on a good objective test: a game of fifty points of three cushion billiards against a good opponent. Playing under the aegis of "Together" I proceeded to average *three per inning*, making no mechanical errors of any kind—a phenomenal performance.

I was not amazed at myself, though I felt a mysterious aura around me; I was merely living perfectly on an inanimate billiard table. But wondering if this test were objective enough, I let a day go by, and on the second day following, playing against a professional, I made the fifty points in fifteen innings, this time an average *slightly better* than three.

A Week of Imperviousness

A week's share of normal pain followed but it was not felt, not recognized, as pain. Pain merely seemed to be a necessary accompaniment of life on earth, salt for the food of joy, spice for the substance of perfection. Work became a bodily function like breathing, almost automatic in the climate of Self-Togetherness.

Time stood still; there were no minutes or hours; everything was enjoyed in an infinity of time. Money was still money but like pain it was there without any bad qualities; its knack for creating unrest was totally missing.

So as one perfect day followed another, the revelation came that this was heaven on earth and with complete clarity I saw that I was reveling in the kind of Perfect Living to which I and all other human beings were naturally entitled.

Temporary Parting

But as the week neared its close, faint disturbances were detectable. The word *Together*, silently spoken, was not producing such luscious and soul-satisfying sighs. The magic wand was losing its wallop. Self-doubt began. Had I been deluded and misled? Had I lost the key? Was my one week of heaven on earth only another wild goose chase in the futile pursuit of happiness?

But an inward voice kept counseling: "Do not despair. Your joy lasted uninterrupted for a full week—that's some kind of a record. *Perfect Living is possible*. Accept this grand sample—and continue your search."

The Thesis Remained

In the weeks that followed it became clear that the thesis which disclosed every man's first aim in life could never again be ignored. The word *Together* had come out of the thesis. I had been *Together* for a week. Now I was *Apart*. If I could recover my Self-Togetherness and keep it permanently, I could be happy forever while still on earth.

And that word *Together* emphasized still another inescapable fact. It proved that the best way for the conscious mind of you and me to communicate with our subconscious sides was through the medium of a *single word*.

One Word Enough as a Push Button

My liaison with the one word *Together* indicated that the subconscious soul is usually willing to accept a single word where it will resist a large number of words. A single little word, uttered without meaning, cannot be a lecture and could hardly be called a suggestion, but the sub-self shows a readiness to heed it because it is not a command or injunction issued by the conscious person.

I had begun to use the word *Together* not to convey meaning as words are ordinarily used, but rather *as a push button or a switch!* I said it quietly, mildly, never thinking of what it meant. I trusted the word so fully, it was no longer a word but rather a device for switching on internal machinery that made me sigh and then, after the sigh, made me feel clean, fearless and content.

Forget About Edison, Steinmetz, Westinghouse

When one flips on an electric light switch in his home, he does not stare at the light bulb and shout a command: "Light up!" He does not review a short course in electricity and elucidate to himself or to others the process by which the current reaches the filament and makes light. He does not think of Edison, Steinmetz or Westinghouse. All he does is flip the switch and *believe the light will follow.*

His objective is clear. He *wants* light. His belief is perfect; he knows the switch will deliver the light he wants. In fact, his belief is so immense that should the switch *fail* to deliver the light, he would be thoroughly surprised and momentarily refuse to believe in the failure.

In my unforgettable week, I had found a switch that delivered Perfect Living. I had worked it exactly as I would an electric light switch. I had wanted the joy it would deliver and believed completely in its powers, though I was unaware of any underlying system or process that responded to the switch and caused the delivery.

And no thought was given to what made the miracle possible. It was only when the magic switch *Together* began to weaken, and finally failed, that I found myself faced with the job of learning the WHY and HOW behind the Miracle.

5

YOUR
UNDERGROUND
FACTORY

Even THOUGH YOU ARE ENTIRELY A *personal* BEING, completely different from an inanimate machine, you are often led to suspect the presence within you of a "set of works" that does things independent of your watchful consciousness.

The subconscious alarm clock that wakes you up at the desired hour is the familiar example. But there are many more.

The Subconscious "Geiger Counter"

You are faced with a problem that involves search, memory, analysis and some detective work. You seldom solve the problem in a minute or an hour. But address it to your subconscious, take your knowing mind off it, and eventually your subconscious machinery, like a Geiger Counter detecting uranium, delivers the answer. Then you say: "That solution is so simple, why didn't I think of it sooner?"

You have seen or heard of a mathematical prodigy. He may

be a boy or a man, able to multiply long and extremely complicated sets of figures in a second, without stopping to write down his calculations. Such people do exist. You say of them: "They are faster than a machine and just as accurate."

Certainly you have dreams. In your dreams images and thoughts get mixed up in a cascade of motion and meaning, sometimes clear, sometimes inexplicable. Often, in a matter of seconds, you dream a story whose action in a world awake might take a week. Where do dreams come from? How exactly are they made? No one knows, but all of us feel they are *manufactured things* coming out of some vague and elusive mechanism inside our very selves.

You Are a Well-Equipped, Modern Plant

The vegetable processes your body goes through in taking in food, getting nourishment, growing and sustaining its balance of health are identical with those of the tree or any other vegetable. The word *plant*, referring to a factory where things are made, comes from the *plant*, meaning vegetable, for the good mechanical factory, in its layout and action, copies the photosynthesis of the vegetable.

You are well acquainted, too, with automatic reflexes, common and visible, which are so certain in their action they may be almost termed mechanical. You yawn and another, seeing you yawn, yawns also. One person in a group, itching, starts scratching and soon others begin scratching with him.

Laughter From a Set of Tools and Dies

All laughter is recognizable; it all seems to come from the same set of tools and dies. You wouldn't ever call it *mechanical*, but still you do know you have a laughing *machine* inside you which springs into action in its own sweet way without ever consulting your intellect or will.

And isn't your whole nervous system a kind of factory, too, with its complicated network of communications carrying sounds and smells, tastes and touches of varying degrees to the brain, an almost infinite number of feelings that all the words in the dictionary are inadequate to describe?

Your eye has been called the perfect camera. Isn't a camera a machine?

But constantly thinking of yourself as a *person,* with freedom to move or not to move, to choose between right and wrong, you properly place yourself on a level high above the *machine.* Conscious of your dignity as a man, you may be too ready to deny the *existence* of the machinery of *your own experience.*

You Are Your Own Experience

For you are your own experience. Everything that ever happened to you, everything you ever thought or imagined, everything you ever dreamed, everything that ever floated by—whether you dreamed it, or felt it, or recognized it as experience, is your true experience and it has never left your possession. You may insist that your only experience is the experience you can call to mind, the skills and abilities you can demonstrate in the clear light of day.

But don't be reckless. Why disown your TOTAL EXPERIENCE, the millions and billions of things that have been *you,* which you cannot remember?

You Have Walked on Water

In imagination, in dreams, in surreal living you have walked on water, floated in air, busted through thick brick walls, conversed in a dozen foreign tongues—but you won't admit it. You have done everything that is in the realm of the possible and everything that is outside the realm of the conventional.

Do not disown your own past. Your infinite experience may be unused, unrecognized, unclaimed, but buried and unseen, it is still *experience*. It is not dead, and being *you*, it cannot leave.

Awaken to this startling news: You are the sovereign superintendent of a vast, immeasurable domain that holds the secret of a perfect life, the fulfillment of all your needs and wants, the true destiny of your whole personality.

You are owner and ruler of an experience factory larger and more potent than any industrial enterprise on earth. This is the factory of your "keeping memory," the feedback computer that forever holds every last trace of the tiniest experience.

Take a Look at This Factory

Because your total life experience cannot be announced or recited out loud and because it has had to stay with you, removed from your conscious mind and your knowable words and acts, *it has gone underground.*

It is the sub-you we have been referring to, your great subsurface, subconscious self. It is your underground factory staffed with hundreds of ingenious machines, of finest design and perfect efficiency, whose complicated workings are still unknown to you.

Most of the machines are idle all of the time because, not knowing they are there, we do not call on them to perform. Once in a while we hear a soundless signal and say of some word or remark: "That rang a bell!" It did! And a machine started to work, to deliver something we wanted or needed.

Natural Functions Divorced From Consciousness

Life, viewed as the *life everyone must live,* is nothing more than the sum total of

Your natural needs
Your distresses
Your desires

The underground machines for taking care of our natural needs have for the most part been kept in fair working order. Digestion, breathing, blood circulation are normal functions of every human body, intended to be purely automatic and dissociated from control of the conscious mind. We do not refer in words to our digestion "machine," our breathing or circulation "machine." But a little reflection should tell us each process operates just like a machine, the only difference being all our parts are of live material, not of metal.

And we do get a highly satisfactory and efficient performance out of all our biological machines, large and small.

Where Trouble Starts

It is only when we get into that phase of life *where body is supposed to work with mind* that trouble starts.

Your hundreds of desires, all now unfulfilled—have you machines within you that are intended to help you achieve these desires, and thus deliver happiness?

Your hundreds of acute distresses—pains, fears, worries, and weaknesses—are there machines anywhere in your personal factory that have a prescribed function for taking you out of misery and into the life of perfection?

In imagination let's descend the stairs to the basement of your personality and see what is there.

Inspect Your Underground Factory

Down here in your subterranean factory we see a marvelous array of amazing machines, of involved and yet simple design.

Half the machines have been designed to help you fulfill your desires; the other half to help you relieve yourself of your distresses.

Each machine long ago was made out of your *experience*. It is perfect in its own special way. If you can switch it on, and if you will believe in it implicitly before and after you have switched it on, it cannot fail. It stands there ready to go to work for you in this very instant, if you will only call on it, trust in it.

It knows its job, it knows you. It knows everything about the desire or distress you are now struggling with and trying to conquer by "old-fashioned" intelligence, passion and hard work.

As Personal as Your Own Heart or Tongue

The machine is ready and willing to take all thinking and all personal effort off your shoulders; it is constituted of a mountain of personal experience, unknown skills, and amazing cleverness. It is yours, all yours, a creature of your own past, as personal as your own heart or tongue.

There it is. If you had been using it as regularly and as unceasingly as you have indeed used your heart and tongue, it would be in perfect working order today. And if you had believed in these desire-fulfilling and distress-relieving machines, trusting them to do their proper work through all your years, life would really be simple and *Perfect Living without effort* would be already in your grasp.

I didn't believe in Perfect Living till I had that week of perfect bliss described previously. It was the short word *Together* that opened my eyes to this push-button theory of Perfect Living. I discovered *Together* was a switch, that by using this word-switch I was turning on hidden, unseen machinery, and the machinery was delivering a physical and psychological effect of boundless rapture.

"Together" Was the Master Switch

What I did not realize at the time, but what my subsequent researches revealed, was that I had accidentally stumbled on the MASTER SWITCH TO MY WHOLE UNDERGROUND FACTORY. For one week, *Together* switched on all the machines. But it was sheer accident. I was starting at the end of the trail instead of at the beginning. It is true that once our underground factories have been put into tip-top working condition, the magic switch "Together" should be able to turn on all the individual machines at once.

But not right away. We must first set out to put each individual desire-fulfillment machine and distress-eliminating machine into order. They are rusty, out of alignment, sprung by neglect and disuse. It will take belief, trust, adjustment and many trial runs before we can restore each machine to working efficiency.

Roll Up Your Sleeves

This rehabilitation process will require work, study and experiment by you; you'll have to roll up your sleeves and get intimately acquainted with each specific switchword that activates the individual machines. And it needn't be work at all—it can be sheer pastime, enjoyment, adventure!

As you begin, you may not be able to give your complete belief to the theory; but do not be disturbed. Your faith will start to snowball as the individual machines, called on by you for special performance, time and again deliver their amazing "miracles."

6

SUBMISSION TO
THE HIGHER POWER

A SHOESHINE STAND IS A STRANGE PLACE TO FIND PEACE. But climb up, and as the boy starts to work on your shoes, a soothing feeling settles over you. You may or may not need the shine; often you get up there because you unconsciously feel the need for a pickup. Of course, you are more than willing to accept the improved appearance of your shoes and as you watch them being shined, you congratulate yourself on your decision to have the work done. But over and above it all, you are enjoying a kind of content and repose you simply cannot buy anywhere else.

On the train, when the Pullman porter shines your shoes overnight, you are pleased when you pick them up in the morning; but you have missed the deeper, richer pleasure of having them shined on your feet, while you looked on in person.

The act of putting yourself in another's hands, of submitting wholeheartedly to the ministrations of the shoeshine boy for ten minutes, makes the big difference. Miraculous peace seems to issue when you surrender your temporary dominion over all matters concerned with yourself, and release yourself to Something Bigger.

The Soldier's Return to Camp

Soldiers on a week-end pass feel it as they return to camp. They have reveled in their liberty and think they never want to go back. But returning, when the camp comes into view, the camp with a new week of labor and disgust ahead, the soldiers feel a sudden rush of resignation and trust, a stilling of inner turmoil; and the camp like a great mother reaches out her arms and clasps her wandering sons to her bosom. Every civilian feels the same way coming home from a vacation; he may have traveled to distant parts and seen thrilling sights, but the sight of "Home, Sweet Home" is always the best of all.

Giving and Forgiving

Giving and forgiving are fine examples of personal submission to something bigger than your conscious mind. Before you can persuade yourself to give anything away—a present, a service, a spiritual gift—you must first "give in." This "giving in," this surrender of selfishness, is recognition of something bigger than your own flimsy equity in the thing given. The sacrifice ought to hurt—but the reverse is true. When you give, you feel noble, never impoverished.

Go around for a day and try excusing everyone you meet, every person you happen to think of. Find some silent praise for the strange faces and bodies you see in the passing throng, the people whom ordinarily you condemn for no good reason.

End Your Personal Boycott

Though there is nothing here to forgive, forgiving brings you joy of divine quality. And how much nicer it is to forgive when there actually *is* something which only you can forgive!

For instance, that store you have declared you would never enter again. They treated you meanly, refused to exchange a wrong purchase, perhaps cheated you. You have boycotted the owners and sworn you will never again give them a penny of your money.

How wonderful it is to abandon this boycott, enter the store again and do business with the very people you despise. This turnabout may please or astonish the storeowner. It does not matter. What does matter is that you have used your right to end a private war. Without rhyme or reason, you have humbled yourself, perhaps subjected yourself to the ridicule of the people you are forgiving. Nonetheless you are the gainer. For no price could be too high to pay for this new uplifted feeling, this release from a mean vow.

To Apologize Is Ennobling

How ennobling it is to apologize to another when you have been in the wrong, and how doubly thrilling it is—if you can bring yourself to do it—to apologize when you know he is as much in the wrong as you.

You cannot belittle yourself in your own eyes when you forgive; you cannot feel anything as a payoff except a great surge of goodness.

The Theory of Submission

It does not matter what that Something Bigger is. It does not matter to what or to whom we submit, just so long as we do submit—without bitterness, without odious comparisons.

Submission never takes away an ounce of your integrity. Every day you submit to the law of gravity, the passing of time, the conventions of society, of law and order. Yet you find no thrill in doing *what you must do*, the things you are denied the choice of *not* doing. But doing what you do not have to do, giving up what you do not have to give up, always makes you a bigger and better person.

You Can Skip Your Morning Bath

You can skip your bath this morning, you can take a cold shower or not—it is up to you. Forget the bath, forget the shower, forget the time and trouble that goes with it. But submit to the bath or the shower, submit to the shock, the water, the cold water. The unpleasantness turns to delight and you emerge from the bath tingling with life and good spirits.

The Many Varieties of Submission

Every motorist, at some time or other in his life, finds himself stuck in a snowdrift or in mud or sand or ice. Though the "Good Samaritan" does not appear every time, you can never forget the instance when a kindly stranger did appear and help push you out of your hole.

The rescue had about it "the touch of the divine" and in a fainter degree you have felt the same touch when a considerate passing motorist informed you your lights were on or off by mistake. The stranger who gave this friendly tip has now passed by, it is too late to thank him. But as you exult in the fine feeling of gratitude for his service, you realize that unconsciously you knew all along your lights were not right.

The Sweetness of Convalescence

Convalescence following a serious illness is one of the sweet-est times in life. The danger is now over; fear and distress are in the past. All there is to do is get well, slowly and surely, and you enjoy every delicious moment of the recovery. Maybe your sickness was brought on by indulgence, excitement, overwork or some other excess. You tried your best to fight it off, to keep on your feet, but at last you had to give in and submit; you went to bed; got sicker still. Then the crisis came and the illness began to subside.

Over the Hill to Oneness

As you get over the hill in a grave illness, a grand feeling of oneness comes to you, a new, indescribable strength in the midst of weakness. You are getting better. You have won a battle against big odds. By submitting to what was necessary, by humbly accepting the care of your doctors and nurses and being obedient to all instructions, you have now become an entirely new person— one with yourself, and one with the world.

To get well is a divine thing, too. You forget about past pain, future work, and simply dwell on the fact that you are on the mend. If there remains in you any desire to fight your sickness, you are still sick. For fighting yourself at any time and in any way is sickness.

PRACTICES IN SUBMISSION

These practices in submission are for the times when you are overwrought, when you feel you cannot cope with your emotional stresses. Your spirits may be depressed, your nerves on edge; irritability, hostility, complaining and fault-finding combine to give you a case of what one sufferer describes as "maggots in the brain."

These ideas are temporary idea pills. They will help restore a measure of normal perspective and tranquillity.

Call the Feeling by Its Most Shocking Name

There is a man or woman whose personality annoys you terribly. You are giving this person too much thinking time and thus robbing yourself of healthy thinking for your own work and living.

You go so far as to say: "I dislike that so-and-so intensely." Go farther. Say: "I HATE THAT PERSON WITH EVERY OUNCE OF HATE ANY HUMAN BEING CAN HAVE!" Of course it is not that bad, but say it anyhow. Say it to yourself. Say it out loud (in privacy) and listen intently to the sound of your own voice as you say it. The native goodness within you will warn you not to hate anyone that much.

But admit the truth of the matter (this is just a practice): If you dislike a person, you HATE him. If you dislike a job, you HATE it. Hate is a form of lunacy, and when anyone hates, he is not just "mad," he is a lunatic and a madman!

Now reflect: Does this person or this thing deserve all this intense feeling? Is he or it important enough to win from you such a costly excess of emotion? In such a state of hate, jealousy or anger, your best resort is to the form of submission known as *artificial elation.*

Artificial Elation

If you are close to drowning or suffocation, your body calls for artificial respiration. Now in your overwrought state, your soul cries for artificial *elation.*

The key is simple: Manipulate the thing which should make you feel bad into making you feel good. By artificially blocking yourself from slipping backwards, you can quickly jump forward!

The material for artificial elation is real handy. Spend a day in using people in your own behalf. The driver ahead suddenly

stops his car without signaling. Should you blow your top? No—
elate! Say: "I feel great, I'm glad he did it." Someone insults you
—either deliberately or by accident. *Elate.* Ordinarily you would
fly off the handle and answer back, or go into your hole and
brood. But here is a chance to turn an insult into something useful. *Elate.* Announce: "I am important enough to be insulted.
This is a great boost to my spirits."

If there is nothing immediately before you to get your "goat,"
recall some "enemy" to mind. Then begin to praise him silently,
to think nothing but good thoughts about him. To turn the faults
of another into material for elation of your own spirit may require
superior skill, but a little practice in the art will bring amazing
results.

Quits a Poor Movie in Five Minutes

You do not have to sit all the way through a poor movie. Many
a wise moviegoer goes to the show alone. He demands the right
to leave the theatre as soon as he finds the movie is no good. He
delights in forfeiting the full admission price to escape from poor
"entertainment." He gets as much kick out of leaving a poor
show as in staying to watch a good one.

If you argue with your doctor, or disobey his instructions,
you deprive yourself of entry into that condition of Self-Togetherness which will provide the fastest cure for your illness. If you
submit to your tourist guide, your will really enjoy your tour.
If you submit to your bus driver, and trust him all the way, praise
him frequently in the silence of your own mind, the roughness of
the ride will be forgotten.

Nearly every submission is a submission of the conscious mind.
When the fault-finding ability of the conscious mind is deliberately shut off, the subconscious actually cheers at the surrender.
This is indeed honor for the subconscious soul, the silent, but
immensely strong workhorse side of the person. Words are not its
business. When words of criticism, revenge, condemnation are

temporarily shut off, your subconscious shows its appreciation by making you feel fine at once.

He Deliberately Humiliates His Conscious Mind

Fleming Johnson, the noted engineer, discloses his special formula for relaxation. Whether he wants to relax in a chair for five minutes or get a full night's perfect sleep, as he sits or lies down he says to his big bloated "stuffed-shirt, self-conscious mind":

> "You're the dumbest guy in the whole
> world—you don't know nothing!"

He makes this drastic announcement to the side of his personality that seeks to exaggerate his problems, work up needless tension. The admission of ignorance releases his big underself from the dungeon of dissatisfaction and self-apartness. By subduing his conscious claims to self-importance, he says in effect: "My great Subconscious, my real self, actually knows everything and I now give it the assignment of releasing me from tension."

He Likened His Inner Storms to Nature's

There is the case of the cranky man who was bothered by everything but the weather. Little children cutting across his lawn threw him into a fit of temper. Imperfections in other people made him rant and roar by the hour. Hypertension was due to take him over and destroy him, if he allowed his crabbiness to run on unbridled.

But a terrible thunderstorm came, his trees were knocked down, his basement flooded and valuable property ruined. What some people would have called disaster merely stimulated him into feeling fine. He saw he could not blame Nature for her outbursts because Nature could have no reason for picking on him in particular.

That storm turned him into philosopher. He began to liken the faults and peccadilloes of other people to Nature's. "They mean no more harm than a minor storm," he admitted. "I'll try to enjoy human storms in the way I enjoy Nature's."

Another "crybaby" type of man was always upset by petty annoyances but never in the least disturbed by any *serious* loss. An accident to his car, the burglary of his home, a serious reverse on the stock market never disturbed him in the slightest.

So he set out to transpose his submission to big setbacks over into the field of petty annoyances. Quoting Nietzsche, "Nothing that is necessary can annoy me," he realized that all the small defects in his fellow men were tiny but necessary evils to be laughed at.

Produce Something, Do Something

The proper function of the subconscious you is to store up experience and ability and then put this ability to work. Your big underself loves work.

Too many of us are given to conscious meditation and postponement of the many things we should be doing. Submit to your subconscious and do something right now. Clean out a cluttered drawer of your desk. Throw away a lot of useless things. Write a personal letter you have been postponing. Pay some bills. Do something, *anything*, so you can temporarily still the discontent inside you.

The Bricklayer Gazes Proudly at His Wall

When the bricklayer gets through with his day's work, he can look back (and he always does) at the part of the wall he built that day, and derive great satisfaction at seeing the results of his work. He has fed his subconscious work hunger.

The office worker misses many such thrills. If your work is not as tangible or as visible as bricklaying, it is a good idea to try to make some of the work visible. Stare at the long overdue letter you have just written. Enjoy the vista of the garage or basement you have just cleaned up. Enjoy the small measure of Self-Togetherness that ensues when your subconscious soul has been served with real work.

Good Work Is a Lot of Fun

And do not be in too much of a hurry when you produce or create. Your subsurface self not only loves work, it especially loves GOOD work. Do not be in too much of a hurry to finish the job —act like the craftsman who always seeks perfection. If you make a bench, there is not much satisfaction for you if it looks ugly, if it lists to one side, if the boards are split. Work carefully, work well, and take your time. The more quality you put into the job, the more thrill there is to it. And your subconscious self is especially grateful to your conscious soul for submitting and not wanting to spoil the production.

Walk Fifty Feet Thinking of Every Step You Take

When you give anybody your full attention to everything he says or does, you honor him immensely and he is drawn to like you at once.

Narcisco Irala, the great Nicaraguan parapsychologist, suggests the following exercise to anyone who is tense or unstrung:

Walk about fifty feet thinking of every step you take, feeling the floor or ground acutely, the rhythm of your body, the tilt of your torso. Notice every small motion and minor physical feeling as you walk.

A few minutes well applied to this simple exercise can pull many a person out of a nervous tail spin. By paying attention to the side of himself engaged in the simple act of walking and noting its surprising subtleties, he automatically takes his conscious mind off itself and submits to a realization of how marvelous his subconscious is in even a small thing.

REMINDER

Getting together with yourself, bringing your two warring sides to an armistice which may lead to permanent peace, is possible. The side of you which most needs to submit is your conscious, talking, visible, audible self. But in humbling your conscious side, you must remember that your subconscious does not know as much about what is good and right in the moral realm as your conscious mind. The subconscious can be a terrible power for evil if let to run unbridled.

It is true that in most cases the subsurface self is the victim of too much ATTEMPTED discipline by the conscious self. True self-discipline should aim at bringing about an armistice between your two warring camps. But before any armistice is possible, an appreciation of the natures and rights of each camp must be felt by the whole person.

"Fanatics Not Wanted"

There is no place for fanatics in the School of Perfect Living. To submit to your great underself is the first big step in understanding this new life, but you must never throw overboard all your conscious knowledge and reasoning faculties. Your personal duties as a member of conventional society, your deference to and respect for the rights of others, your obedience to civil and moral law receive their proper balance not from the Great Big You Underneath but directly from your rational faculties.

Sex maniacs, rapists, sex deviates are people who let the subconscious get the upper hand and run away with the entire person. Alcoholism is an ill that begins with the nice "self-together" feeling that the first few drinks engender.

Most excesses, even overwork, are products of the subconscious machinery in the man, telling him to keep it up, keep it up, overdo, overdo it. To break any habit like too much smoking, overeating, or overuse of sleeping pills, the conscious man must step forward, get on speaking terms with his great underself, and convince the whole person that he must begin to *taper* off—not shut off the habit abruptly, but gradually. All gradations, all moderations come from the conscious mind.

An Emerson Paradox

Ralph Waldo Emerson, great transcendentalist teacher and writer, had two favorite sayings that at first thought seem to conflict:

> Whoso would be a man must be a non-conformist.
> Be very careful what you set your heart upon for you will surely have it.

But notice that Emerson, while urging everyone to strike out in new directions and avoid the beaten path of convention, stressed the all-important phrase: "BE VERY CAREFUL WHAT YOU SET YOUR HEART UPON."

"Be very careful" means: Let reason balance your personality. "What you set your heart upon" is the wild goal the subconscious finally seizes as its own private property, and when the subconscious is allowed to run wild without any check from reason, it can easily accomplish the whole undoing of the person.

"Love At First Sight"

A very handsome young man meets a very beautiful young girl. It is love at first sight, and true love is, of course, a great subconscious love. Handsome Harry sees only the beauty in the girl;

doesn't notice her poor education or the broken English used by her foreign parents. Careless Caroline falls for Harry's fine college education as well as his beauteous looks, but doesn't mind that he drinks and gambles too much. Here love has been allowed to go its way unbridled and in a short time the marriage of Harry and Caroline is on the rocks.

Too often the subconscious, promising great everlasting joy and happiness, lets you down abruptly. Pure reason and logic, of course, can't get you anywhere all by themselves, but all by themselves they do not subject one to sudden disillusionments and shocking letdowns.

"Repulsive Talker"

Raymond X. calls himself a "compulsive talker." He knows he keeps talking all the time; likes to say he "can't stop." The compulsions of his subconscious, it is true, have made him a tireless talker, but lack of proper guidance from his conscious mind has made him not only "compulsive" but rather "repulsive." For all his talk is about one thing—a strange water diet wherein one regains health by drinking water for 40 days, and eating nothing. If Ray had a hundred subjects to talk about and could guide each subject toward an appropriate audience, his compulsion not only would be overlooked, but Ray would be known as a most interesting conversationalist. But he still goes on talking *ad nauseam*.

Thomas Wolfe

Thomas Wolfe, the famous novelist from Asheville, N.C., had terrific subconscious drive in his writing, and in his short life wrote several million words that never reached print. He once confessed he wrote in such great volume "To get the words out of my system." Like other great artists in history, Wolfe allowed his conscious mind to direct his great subterranean urges toward a worthy target—fine art in writing. The quality of his output more than made up for his "compulsive writing."

Lack of Conscious Direction
Can Mean Sudden Death

Glenn McShane, an expert upholsterer, has to drive great distances in calling on homes where he takes measurements. Glenn tells me he often drives for 20 minutes on the freeway at 70 miles an hour *without ever seeing the road,* or being able to say what he saw, did, or thought of in those 20 or more miles. His subconscious machinery is automatically driving the car for Glenn. Other drivers attest they do the same thing themselves on non-stop highways—go for 20 miles without "consciously feeling a thing."

These automatic feats are truly sensational, and indicative of what the sub-self is capable of without any help from the conscious mind. But in a "weapon" as lethal as an automobile, such automation should not be indulged in. No sane person would drive a car while half asleep, and yet with the subconscious entirely in charge of a speeding automobile he comes close to taking the same awful risk. Let a touch of conscious mind stay with you when you're behind the wheel.

All Excesses Need Help From the Conscious

Hypertension is one of the greatest sicknesses of Americans. Here's a young suburbanite, not used to digging, but when he digs in the yard, you would think he is trying to reach China. He puts everything he has into every vicious thrust of the spade, and tires very quickly. Another obese man eats so fast and so nervously he shows no sign of pleasure but rather looks like he is merely trying to destroy the food in front of him. Another smokes one cigar after another so fast and furiously his friends call him "the ash manufacturer."

Bill, the barber, confesses "his mind never stops working,"

and says it feels like he has "maggots in his brain." All this excessive nervousness indicates a complete absence of any checkrein on the subconscious. And because the person involved commits no crime, that might be punished in court, the excess runs on and on.

Invite the Conscious In

If, like the barber, you can recognize your trouble and bravely announce it to yourself, you have made a start toward balancing your underself with your conscious self.

Another good approach is to count your abuses while they are happening under your eyes. If you can't sleep because your mind is working too fast and freely, say: "Off," and then count each added thought that creeps in unwanted.

Try to remember all the times, when you were assailed by laziness, with the conscious chastising you because the subconscious was doing nothing. Force yourself to include the elements of truth, beauty and goodness into every project and never let your subconscious take your conscious mind off the esthetic side of every activity.

To sum up: The conscious is still the office boy of the personal corporation of which the subconscious is the president. But get the president to listen to the office boy occasionally when his services are clearly needed.

7

TESTING

THE WORDS

OF POWER

Self-TOGETHERNESS IS THE ANSWER TO ALL OF LIFE'S challenges.

Togetherness of husband and wife, togetherness of the children with their parents, has been preached up and down the land as a practical means of achieving family unity and tranquillity. Psychologists urge it and give much evidence of its efficacy. Religious spokesmen exhort: "Go to Church together. The family that prays together, stays together."

But Perfect Living enthusiasts have seen countless achievements that far outdistance, in quality and scope, the miraculous effects of togetherness in the family. This is why we are so anxious to submit the system to an immediate test. And the test for you can be very simple:

TRY THE SWITCHES!

If you are inclined to be nervous and excitable without good reason, your friends will tell you to relax. (But they never bother to tell you HOW to relax.) Relaxing is really a combination state produced by the action of several of your underground experience machines. When you have restored your whole underground factory to perfect working order, you can flip the master switch with the easy word "Together" and relax to a fare-thee-well at once. But first oil up, correct, realign the parts of each individual machine.

A Mild Relaxer

Try out this one mild form of relaxation, a sigh of relief. A sigh will not relieve you of all of your tensions, but it certainly will help you a little on the road to relaxation.

Right now—do you want to sigh?

Silently say the switchword that produces a sigh:

"HO!"

If, wanting to sigh, and appreciating the immediate profit in a sigh, you silently say "Ho," you will surely sigh, or else you are so relaxed you have no need for relaxation at all. "Ho" is such an effective switch because your conscious mind does not try to follow its meaning. This is the way to apply all the switches—try not to think of what the switchword means in English.

Consciously declare you want to sigh, admit you have a good need for a sigh, and silently say "Ho." Did you not sigh? Try it again and you will sigh again. The immediate result of this simple test may startle you a little but do not turn your back on its magic. Repeating such a small test will serve to build up your faith in the theory of Perfect Living.

To Stand Up Straight

Sometimes the name of a living person can be an effective switch. Are you inclined to slump, not stand up to your full height? Remember a friend or acquaintance you admire for standing perfectly straight, with a posture that commands universal admiration. Say the name of that person to switch on your posture-restoring machine. It may be a man named "Roy," tall not handsome, but because he stands so straight he is more than handsome. You know such a person, man or woman. Silently say: "Roy" or "Grace." Notice that you instantly pull yourself to your full height, stomach in, straight as a rod.

Some psychologists may say: "This is merely a case of suggestion through example." Let us grant they are right. The experience machines of Perfect Living have no fight with suggestion, with conscious science, or any known means of producing good results. The machines will operate with auto-suggestion, chemistry, physical science, just as readily as with unseen, unnamed forces. The big point is this: *the switch works.*

He Switched on Instant Politeness

Most of the switchwords are verbs probably because verbs are words of direct action. But the switch can be any other part of speech.

The switchword for politeness is "Tiny." An associate discovered it one night as he sat in his comfortable living room chair writing down notes and ideas on Perfect Living. At the height of his comfort, he realized his wife was busy washing dishes in the kitchen. "Hard work after a hard day! I should be more polite to my own wife," he mused.

Wondering about a good switchword to turn on his politeness-manufacturing machine, he whispered "Tiny" to himself, and sprawled a little deeper into his chair. After a moment he automatically arose and proceeded to the kitchen. To help wifey finish the dishes? No. Not even knowing what he was about, he walked up to her, removed her eyeglasses, took them to the bathroom—without saying a word all the time—washed the lenses and dried them. Returning to the kitchen he put them back on her face, still silent as if in an automatic trance. A moment later he returned to his seat in the living room. She followed him almost immediately and exclaimed: "That was the most polite thing that ever happened to me in my whole life!"

It Is Real Fun to Be Polite

You can easily sample the pleasures of politeness. Tell yourself, your whole self, that right at this moment you are going to be extraordinarily polite. Make the test whether human beings are nearby or not. With your politeness objective crystal clear, silently say "Tiny." Let yourself go. Plan nothing, think of nothing. If other people happen to be near, you will walk up to them and say or do something so polite they will be amazed.

You may sidle over to the telephone, call a friend or stranger, and in language fit for the gods, thank him, congratulate him, or merely by greeting him make him feel as if he is the most important person in the world. Or you may reach for pen and paper and write a thrilling letter in the most gracious terms, perfectly phrased and surfeited with courtesy and affection.

It is fun to be polite. Try "Tiny." Keep it up and you will be the most distinguished man in town.

To Prolong a Fine Feeling

Another test. For this one you must be feeling good at the start. If not, wait till you get a good sleep, a fine meal or a surprise gift that tickles and pleases. Then the switchword to prolong the good feeling is "Stretch." Throw the switch and see what happens. You find yourself dwelling on the cause or causes of the good feeling instead of wasting your attention on new distractions and annoyances. While you cannot prolong the good feeling forever, "Stretch" will extend it.

Familiar Actions Can Be Switches

As you read this, force yourself to SMILE. Now hold that smile and keep it on your face while you think of your worst enemy, the man whose every action you hate and condemn. While still smiling, try to HATE, try to envy, try to plot revenge or harm. You cannot if you are still smiling. This test is a fine example of how your invisible experience-machinery can neutralize the worst poisons of the human personality.

A similar switch is the one that turns on your writing machinery. Nearly everyone hates to write. Some people would rather dig ditches than write the ordinary letters they owe to their dear friends.

The switch for writing is the action: GIGGLE. It is rather foolish to giggle at any time, especially when you do it on purpose. But think of that long-postponed letter, force yourself to giggle, and you can expect some action. The need exists—you definitely *owe* that letter to someone. Giggle and continue giggling. Giggle and see yourself reach for the writing materials. Giggle as you start the letter. Giggle as you write each line. Giggle all the way through. It will be a wonderful letter; and if it is an essay, an article or bit of verse, it will be thrilling to write and thrilling to read.

Help Yourself to Generous Snacks
of Perfect Living

Another fine exercise is reading parts of this book, thinking and talking about the push-button theory. Don't the ideas you find here do something to you? Boost your spirits? Loosen you up? Suggest hope that there at last may be a way to conquer the troubles of life? Open the book anywhere and inhale its message deeply.

"Together" Has Magic

All of the people who have listened to all the angles of Perfect Living and its push button theory have sought to cooperate in studies and experiments of their own. Some have gone off half-cocked and, forgetting all the other attitudes and requisites, merely used the word "Together" in all of their tests.

Strangely, though "Together" should come last, it has worked many sensational results when used first. It may be that "Together" is the first step to intrigue you into a complete study of the science of Perfect Living. As you play your next game of golf, say "Together" before every shot and all through the round. One man did it and broke par for the first time in his life. Another less-than-average bowler tried "Together" and bowled his first 600 series with three strings of five strikes in a row.

"Together" Helps Him Sell

Grant Francis Shay, one of the Midwest's top premium salesmen, is a remarkable exponent of the "Together" principle in his contact with customers. If you had the privilege of playing golf with Shay, it would be a revelation how enjoyable the game (which to most novices is rather stressful) can be.

Golfer Shay instantly makes you feel together with yourself, together with your partner, and so together with the course that it seems to belong to *you*. Every hole is an expedition into more Self-Togetherness, relaxation and enjoyment. Shay takes you around the fairways and greens as if he were introducing you to different subdivisions of heaven itself.

And Shay will confide that, whether selling or entertaining, he all the while keeps on saying "Together" silently and confidently. You, too, can repeat "Together" generously for a minute, an hour, or a whole day. Do it and see what happens.

8

HOW
TO FIND
LOST TREASURES

Reach: AS YOU GO ABOUT YOUR DAILY TASKS, YOU often mislay a certain object with which you are working. The time comes when you need the object and to your consternation you cannot find it. Ridiculous! You just had the thing in your hands. It should be right in front of you, but it isn't. This inanimate article couldn't walk away on its own power and hide from your sight—but where is it?

Where on earth did you put it? Where were you exactly when you last had it in your hands? You fall back on your conscious memory and by a clean-cut process of ratiocination you attempt to *reason* yourself into finding the misplaced article. Sometimes in such a situation reason does work; very often it does not.

You Know and You Don't Know

Still pursuing your search, you stop and analyze yourself. A voice within openly states that you *should* know and you *do* know where the object is. You are sure you know, but you cannot announce this knowledge out loud.

Now the fugitive article becomes a challenge. You get excited You declare you will not let it elude you; the heat of passion is added to the search. With enough drive and passion you may ultimately find it—and again you may not. But when your desire for the lost article reaches the stage in which it is something more than a mere wish, you feel a stirring and a churning of forces within you, prompting you to try harder. Examine your state and you must honestly admit you are a victim of *Apartness*. If you were together with yourself in this search, you would have had the article long ago. Your Apartness is actually keeping you from finding it.

"Don't Stop Now, Keep Going"

The stirring force inside you which says: "Don't stop now, keep going!" is actual notice from your underground factory that the special machine for finding lost articles is ready to go into action. Your conscious experience has failed you, but a world of subterranean experience is still available. All that the machine asks is that you flip the switch that sets it in motion.

Experiments have shown that the word-switch for the special experience machine which finds lost articles is: "*Reach*."

Your objective is clear. You know what it is you are looking for. You believe that one part of you knows where it is. So just say "Reach" and flip the switch. Do not think of the meaning of the word "Reach," simply say it silently without considering its meaning. Flip this word-switch in much the same way you flip an electric light switch. *But keep clearly in mind just what you want to find.*

Now abandon all your conscious thoughts and analyses. Let your body go limp, let your mind rest. Prepare to be a mere automaton instead of a thinking person. Suddenly you find yourself moving in a strange way to a strange place. Lo and behold you push your arm into a strange pile of papers, or open a strange box, or pull a strange drawer, or kick a strange object, and then—almost immediately—the lost article appears right in front of you!

BETTER Than Reason or Common Sense

You did it. *You* found it. A stronger, better part of you than your rational mind, a machine of your own experience, designed for this specific job, did the trick where more "reasonable," more "sensible" methods failed.

In *one hundred* case histories of experiments conducted for finding articles that could not be located by conscious reasoning or memory, there were very few failures.

Took a Day to Locate "Lost" Magazine

One participant reported what at first appeared to be a failure. He was searching for a certain magazine which he was "sure" was in the basement of his home. Unable to find it by the usual method, he resorted to the word-switch system, asking his experience machine for help. For ten minutes he moved around aimlessly, impassively, mindlessly—as he should under the system. But no magazine turned up. Then an inner voice seemed to say: "Give up the search; you can't find it now." He quit.

But next day, downtown in his office, he found the magazine on his desk! Of course, the machine couldn't produce the magazine in his basement—it wasn't there. It couldn't move him downtown at the moment—it was too far away. But all the while it knew where the magazine was; while the man's conscious mind did not know.

The only magic you are asked to believe in is the magic of your own *experience*. If you were handling something and somehow it got lost, that was experience. That was *your* experience— no one else's. The experience is still inside you; there is no possible way for it to get lost, it has to remain with you. If your conscious mind can no longer manage or manipulate it, as it does other experience, that is no reason you need surrender your ownership of the experience.

You Against Yourself

When we examine the incident of the mislaid article, we can find out a great deal about the two conflicting sides of ourselves. Certainly you never mislay an article "on purpose"—that would be sheer idiocy. But stop! In the midst of your frantic search, don't you find yourself accusing yourself of stupidity, or inefficiency, or trouble-making? Don't you feel foolish and frustrated? A mistake is a mistake, sure, and you make plenty of them; but though we all like to consider our mistakes impersonal accidents, we know full well that if a mistake is anything, it is *entirely personal*. It came from us, *we* did it. It is a blow, a setback, a penalty which, perversely and inexplicably, we administer to ourselves.

Mistakes in Living

Here we see clear evidence of the human addiction to Apartness. Some people make a lot more mistakes than others; inevitably they suffer an extra share of Apartness, and the discontent and self-castigation that goes with Apartness. If any person could go through life without ever making a mistake, he would undoubtedly be a Together Person, and a completely happy person. But Apartness tempts and lures us into hundreds of mistakes every day. "Little" mistakes we may call them, but they are all mistakes in *living*, and therefore serious and costly.

Before the word-switch "Reach" can turn on your finder machine, you must *submit*. You must believe in your own experience, you must believe in your own self, you must believe that you are not two separate selves, but one only. This is submission to *Something Bigger*, your own ideal *Togetherness*.

When you are together with yourself, the very experience that was created out of the mistake you made is now ready to correct the mistake and undo the harm that you imposed on yourself. The machinery is there; acknowledge its presence, its efficiency. Use it properly and it cannot fail.

This Machine Easy to Test

The experience machine for finding lost or misplaced articles is one of the easiest to test for the simple reason that many of us have a need for it several times each day.

The classic example is the absent-minded professor who keeps searching for his eyeglasses and is finally told they are where they should be—right on his own nose. But literally millions of people who use eyeglasses for reading constantly find themselves looking for the "case for my glasses."

It is always nearby but that doesn't help the searcher much. He looks in the usual places, his pocket, his desk, his table. No glasses. He tries to recall where he last was standing or sitting when he took his glasses out of the case—but this system does not always work. *He knows deep down in his heart* where the glasses are and that makes the situation all the more maddening since his intelligent memory refuses to help out.

In Pocket, Wastebasket, Cigar Box, Grocery Bag

Some reports after experimenters used the switch "Reach":

"Believe it or not I found the case in my own pocket inside my coat and next to my body."

"I had to leave for the train in three minutes, tried everything and could not put my hands on the case. Finally, I said 'Reach.' WANT was there because I simply HAD to leave at once. I let myself go, walked over to the wastebasket and found the case for my glasses among the wastepaper."

" 'Reach' brought me to the case for my glasses nicely placed in my cigar box with the smokes."

" 'Reach' drove me to the bag of groceries and I found the key to my house there."

Found Court Jester in His Attic

An artist wanted a picture of a court jester. He searched through his "morgue" for a good hour and found none there. He was still sure he had such a picture somewhere in the house. Said "Reach," picturing his objective clearly. Immediately he was impelled to mount the stairs to his attic. His eye fell on a big thick book there, a relic of his student days. "I will open the book on page 567," he announced to himself, "why I don't know, but it is going to be page 567." He did—and found his picture of the court jester on page 567.

It was no miracle. His machine for finding lost articles knew all along where the court jester was. It was merely a matter of putting the machine to work.

The Twice-Mislaid Screwdriver

Another experimenter reported: "I had misplaced my screwdriver and needed it at once. Said 'Reach!' I was automatically prompted to drift over to a ledge on my basement wall. Heaved a sigh of relief, now consciously remembering here was the spot where I had left the screwdriver. But no screwdriver! The system failed? 'No,' said something inside, 'try again.'

"Again I said 'Reach!' Still submissive and believing, I was carried to a box of miscellaneous objects lying on the floor. The screwdriver was there and I HAD NOT PUT IT THERE. But while I had been working in the basement my brother had also been working there. It was he who put the screwdriver in the box, but my experience machine had unconsciously heard him drop it there and knew where to guide me to find it."

They Call Him "Mind Reader"

The details of Perfect Living were given to a young insurance salesman of a high I.Q. rating. He has fun demonstrating it because the switch "Reach" makes possible some sensational performances bigger and better than could be seen in a show.

One day he asked the Chief File Clerk in his office what was troubling her. She was in dire need of finding a certain contract and was about convinced it was lost or destroyed. My friend said "Reach" silently, and then out loud and with a playful smile pointed to the bottom file drawer and said, "Pull open that file drawer, it will be the last document in the file."

"I've already looked there and it could not be there anyhow because it could never have been filed there," she asserted. But she opened the drawer in disgust, pulled out the last document, and sure enough she had the contract she wanted. My friend swears he had no previous knowledge of seeing the document in the file; in fact, he had never been permitted to use the file. "I just blurted out what my finding machine told me to say," he explains.

And to make the show even better, on three more occasions he announced the location of other "missing" documents which had had the Filing Department in an uproar of frantic searching. They call the young salesman "Mind Reader" around the office, they suspect him of tricky showmanship. But all he is doing is giving them flashes of Perfect Living.

Solving Problems While Asleep

If you are faced with a complex and serious problem, you know it is good business to wait overnight, "to sleep on it," before coming to a decision. Very often, without any help from the word-switch "Reach," you do arrive at the correct solution merely by "sleeping" on the problem.

That is your subconscious thinking the details over while you are actually asleep. If the problem is big it is always good to wait before acting. And it is even better to say clearly and meaningfully to yourself: "I want to solve this problem correctly;" thoroughly convince yourself that you have a machine for doing it in your subterranean factory, and then turn on the machine by saying "Reach" without thinking of the meaning of the word.

Finding the Key That "Unlocks" the Buyer

This tip has been given to many salesmen to use when they meet up with tough, hard-to-crack buyers—Say to yourself: "I want to find the key which will unlock this man." Then switch on your finding machine with "Reach."

Fifty percent of these heeders have reported astounding success. The conversations have suddenly veered into archery, bowling on the green, international relations, celestial space, bricklaying, and other strange and intriguing alleys of human activity.

The same experience machine which finds lost or mislaid articles solves problems, creates new ideas, produces inventions, contrives escapes, finds vocations in life—all without any invocation of miraculous or preternatural "powers."

9

THE
SWITCH
THAT BATTLES PAIN

Who IS TO SAY ANYTHING IS IMPOSSIBLE? BY AGREE-
ment men have decided that complete and permanent happiness is impossible on earth and no individual has ever
demonstrated to the satisfaction of scientists that he can be truly
happy all the time. Yet, in contradiction to the impossibility of
happiness, we all find ourselves still searching for it, for the magic
wand that will produce it, for the secret formula that may un-
cover it.

Keep your "I'm from Missouri" attitude, regard your underground experience factory as a mere assumption, and remain as
skeptical as you want about the ability of a simple word to switch
on an unseen personal machine. You needn't believe any of the
case histories and events related here. But if you will only keep

your mind open, sooner or later you will begin a few tests and experiments of your own; and then your belief may be forthcoming.

He Cuts His Toenails, Then Takes a Trip

I have a friend who insists that every time he trims his toenails (once about every two months) *he invariably finds himself taking a trip.* Whether the trip is needed or not, it always results!

When President Theodore Roosevelt needed a shot of energy, he went to the wash bowl and washed his hands.

Millions of women, when feeling low and depressed, unconsciously contrive to buy a new hat or dress to buck up their spirits. Most of us know that when we put on our best suit of clothes, we immediately feel better. Whether such simple actions switch on machines, and whether the switches or the machines exist or not, we will all admit that a favorable result ensues.

There is a machine in your subterranean factory expressly designed to relieve you of *pain.* The switch which actuates this machine and starts it off on its grand mission of relief is the word CHANGE.

Do You Want to Lose Your Headache?

If you have a pain you want to chase away, state the pain formally and clearly to yourself, e.g., "I have a headache and I want to get rid of it at once!" (Please be sure you *want* to get rid of this pain. Some people enjoy their pains and would rather retain them to talk about and keep attention on themselves.) It will, of course, be better—*it will be perfect,* in fact—if you will believe that by merely saying "Change" and wanting to get rid of the pain, the pain will vanish almost instantly. But *your belief* at this point may be too much to ask.

Let us examine a few reports from our experimenters:

Cinder Rendered Harmless

"I had just left my office to go to an all-day meeting, a convention in town. I was on the sidewalk for only a minute when some sharp object entered my eye. Instead of rubbing the eye or pulling the lids, as one often does when the pain is terribly acute, I closed the eye gently, telling myself I wanted the object removed at once because I had to spend several hours at the convention.

"Then I said 'Change' without thinking of the meaning of the word; all I thought of was my acute need to get the eye back to normal. A few seconds later I said 'Change' again, and rested a moment. Then I slowly opened my eye—AND FOUND THE TERRIBLE PAIN HAD GONE. I gave the eye no further treatment, I even refrained from touching it with my handkerchief.

"After spending practically the whole day at the convention, I arrived home about twelve hours later and in preparing for bed happened to brush my eye with my hand, and the STABBING PAIN RETURNED. I went to a mirror and succeeded now in taking out the offending object. IT WAS A CINDER ONE-EIGHTH INCH IN DIAMETER, and it had been in some portion of the eye pocket, insensitive to pain, since morning. My own pain-relieving machine, properly treated to do its proper work, had pushed the cinder into some soft pouch and kept it there, unhurting, till I was able to remove it consciously."

The Black Bug Had a Quarter-Inch Wingspread

A housewife reports: "Coming out of a store onto the street a bug flew in my eye. I knew it was a bug from the course of its flight and its soft and watery feel. I said 'Change,' closed the lids slowly, waited a moment and said 'Change' again. All pain and discomfort vanished immediately. On arriving home I took a magnifying glass and examined my eye in the mirror.

"A black bug, very flimsy in body but more than an eighth of an inch long and with twice that wingspread, WAS TRAPPED BETWEEN THE HAIRS OF MY EYELID in a most ingenious layout. THAT BUG WAS IN MY EYE for a few seconds, and the word 'Change' switched on the machine which has the job of taking care of such emergencies. I am sure the bug was alive when it entered my eye. I am not sure the trap of my own eyelids killed it—merely held it out of reach of doing harm to my eye. I was so elated when I pulled Mr. Bug out of his trap I did not examine him further."

Pipefitter Controls Gout Pains

From a pipefitter: "I was suffering from high blood pressure and the doctor found my uric acid content was way above the normal reading. Prescribing some gout medicine for me, he happened to say laughingly, 'Right now you ought to have the biggest and most painful big toe in the whole world.'

"Two days later an excruciating stab of pain hit my big toe and I suddenly feared I was about to learn the agony of gout.

"But I said, 'Change' and the pain left in a second. Five minutes later it returned. Again I said 'Change,' not thinking of the meaning of the word and not commanding myself in any way, and the pain vanished instantly. My automation machines worked so fast on this gout threat I am convinced that no drug or physical treatment could ever have been as effective."

Men From Missouri Converted

Since pain is such a common experience with all of us, "Change" has probably registered with more experimenters than any other switch. This test appeals to the "show me" side of all people. They will give the theory of Perfect Living this test when they find medicines and other treatments do not help. These "Men from Missouri" have cooperated on many other experiments. The pain-relieving machine and the switchword "Change" have made them believers.

Forty Headaches Banished

Over forty cases of people suffering from severe headache (not chronic, but sudden headache) on saying "Change" and trusting directly to personal cybernetics show immediate banishment of headache. Some of the headaches departed automatically. The significant thing in half of the other cases is this: The switchword "Change" plus belief and want drove them to reach for the seltzer bottle containing antacid. They were curing their pain by conscious means? Not necessarily, for many of them report: "I should have tried a seltzer drink to kill the headache but did not think of it at the time. The Perfect Living system made me think of it and obeying the impulse I found it was just what I needed."

At this point we should make clear that the total you, the Self-Together You, includes not merely your subconscious and subsurface selves but, importantly, your CONSCIOUS SELF. And the finest part of that conscious self is often used in the workings of your underground machinery.

He Cures Himself of Hay Fever

A hay fever victim, with a history of twenty-five years of seasonal agony, hearing of the Perfect Living theory, applied himself to this experiment. His want was prodigious; he had reached the end of his "distress rope," and felt he could not go on. His belief was questionable because he had tried every cure under the sun, to no avail.

The Perfect Living Counselor said to him, "Your affliction is too awful to expect you to believe that a simple word like 'Change,' setting off an invisible machine, can rid you of this disease where other methods have failed. But say it anyhow when you feel the next attack coming on." *It worked*.

Not on the first try completely. But he kept on repeating and wanting and semi-believing at the start of each sneeze or noseblowing. From the very first time he said "Change" he never experienced another acute attack. Progressive results increased his belief, and for seven years he has been COMPLETELY CURED OF HAY FEVER.

He cured himself using his own machines of experience. Some of this experience was highly conscious, such as the unique practices he resorted to in finding a new way to sneeze when sneezing time approached.

Does the System Always Work?

Pain is universally prevalent and has a multiplicity of phases. If the switchword "Change" never failed, if it perfectly did the job it is prepared by nature to do, then all sickness would vanish from the earth.

200 Successes and 1000 Experiments

Two hundred people have experimented with "Change." About a thousand specific applications of this switchword have been examined. A good two hundred of these tests have routed specific pains without doctors' aid and without any prescribed medicines.

Admit the eight hundred failures; but never blame the system if WANT IS MISSING, IF BELIEF IS MISSING, if the switchword has been uttered meaningfully, or if some other error in technique is present.

What about the two hundred successes? None of these cases can be explained by any other system than Perfect Living, which, when properly applied, produced a magical state of Self-Togetherness, giving each rusty, neglected, pain-relieving machine a fair chance to get rolling.

He Burped Himself Out of the Pain in His Chest

Report: "For several hours I was experiencing an annoying pain in the left side of my chest. Could it be my heart? No, a recent cardiogram showed my heart to be O.K. Very annoying. What should I do? I remembered the switchword 'Change' which you gave me for pain. I really wanted to get rid of this pain in the chest because it had lingered so long and, while not sharp or excruciating, was most annoying. Because you had partially sold me on your theory, I had a measure of belief. So I said: 'Change.' Instantly I found myself burping, and the burping continued for several minutes. When the burping stopped, the pain had gone for good."

Comment: It is pretty difficult to burp *on purpose,* unless the subject uses a chemical or physical agent of some kind. But the real under-you knows how to do many things the conscious self cannot do "on purpose!"

Sometimes burping can be begun by an outside suggestion, such as seeing or hearing another person burp. In the above case, which was checked carefully, there was no outside person nearby. But the significant thing is that, outside person or no outside person, *the pain stopped and did not return.*

10

A MAGIC WORD
TO TAKE YOU PLACES

On: YOU HAVE OFTEN FOUND YOURSELF IN A SITUATION where you need transportation immediately. You have no car. There is no bus in sight. You will now settle for a cab but all the passing cabs are loaded with passengers. You are late already—you simply have to get to your destination at once. How to do it? The switchboard for transportation is "ON."

Here the emergency has created a clean-cut *want*. You want to get somewhere because you *have* to. The objective is just as clear; you know what your destination is, you know where you must go immediately. But *belief* has been temporarily shattered by the non-appearance of any transportation aid, and precious time whirls by to increase your disbelief.

In any such transportation crises, it is all important to believe. Perhaps a recitation of many near miracles that happened to others will cause you to test the magic of the switchword "ON."

Successful Use of "On"

These incidents all happened in the vicinity of 95th and Wood Street, Chicago, the Beverly Hills Depot of the Rock Island suburban trains.

"I have often arrived at the depot and found myself with no apparent means of transportation to my home some three miles west. Too far to walk; suburban bus service very inadequate; cab service sparse. Sometimes I have been up against a deadline and in a dire need of getting home without delay, without waiting. In such emergencies I have used the transportation switchword 'ON' with unbelievable success. And I cannot remember a single failure in any such emergency. I can remember at least ten successes and will report a few here.

Good Samaritan Unrecognized

"One day I got off the train early in the afternoon—a bad time for the suburban bus. I was late for an appointment at home. I couldn't try to walk the three miles. So I silently said 'On' as I stepped down from the train.

"At the curb a car was waiting for me. 'Step in, Mr. Friendly,' said the young man driver, 'I'm taking you home.' I did not recognize him but refrained from saying so. He talked like a long-lost brother, all about my family and me. I still couldn't place him. But I was satisfied to get the lift—no questions asked.

"When he discharged me at my house, I couldn't resist asking his identity. His name was Joseph Gallagher, the son of an old friend. He had driven me four miles out of his way.

Standing Room Only

"On another occasion, at the same place, I said 'On' for transportation. It worked—all too well. A milk truck stopped and the driver, Whitey Dubec, a young man I had known since childhood, beckoned me in. There was no provision for riders in this truck, and I had to stand up, crouched against the roof of the truck, all the way home. But I got there in jig time!

Rocky Seemed to Come Out of the Ground

"Trucks are transportation and the system of Perfect Living, when properly used, delivers what you want. On another day I said 'On,' seeing no transportation in sight, but Rocky, an old friend in the roofing business, suddenly appeared as if out of the ground and drove me home in his open truck, which did have an extra seat for a passenger.

A Test Driver Showed Up From Nowhere

"Next time I was driven home, it was Ambrose O'Connell who appeared from nowhere. I had not seen Ambrose in about eight years. As he drove me home, he said, 'I'm a test driver for Nash, I now live in Wisconsin, and I am on my way home. I don't know why I came over 95th St. today; something seemed to say, "It's a good road for a test!"'

Four Different Offers From Four Different Drivers

"Another time, the train was getting into 95th St. at a very poor time for public transportation. Yet my need was acute. While still on the platform of the train, I silently said 'On' four times. As I alighted, *four different drivers in four different cars*, stopped for the gates, hailed me: 'Want a ride home?' One was my brother, John, in his own car. One was my nephew, Jack, in his own car. Another was a neighbor. The fourth car had a driver I did not know from Adam. I thanked them all and jumped into my brother's car just as the gates lifted, and not a second was lost."

A Nice Substitute

Other reports are just as amazing: "Flipping the magic switchword 'On,' a young girl driver, friend of my daughter, tooled her big Cadillac almost to my feet: 'My father was supposed to be on that train, but he isn't,' she said, 'So I'll drive you home instead!'"

Maybe the reader is inclined to think that the drivers referred to are regular users of the road in question, so that the percentage of seeing friends waiting would be coincidence. Or perhaps a skeptic might remark, "These people may be so well known that any driver would recognize them and offer a lift."

But such a theory cannot begin to explain the incidents.

Got a Ride but Dinner Was Late

A commuter said "On" once, and a car traveling in the opposite direction (East) to which he wanted to go, made a U turn farther down the block; coming back, the woman driver called out, "Hop in, I'm late for dinner as it is, but you look like you need transportation badly and I'm taking you home." He accepted automatically with never a thought of muttering the usual cliché: "This is an imposition." (When Perfect Living faces you, don't argue—accept it!) The Good Samaritan was Eunice C. But afterwards she was bawled out by her husband, his friend John. "Our dinner was an hour late, all on account of you," he was told.

When setting your transportation machine to work with the switch "On," you should not appeal for help to any specific person or try to think of a particular Good Samaritan. Leave everything to the machine, and believe.

Picked Up by His Congressman

Says one traveler, "Congressman Ed Kelly picked me up and drove me home one day. 'First time I have been on 95th St. in six months,' he said."

Wanted to See Oak Lawn

Willie Milord, school teacher, a lifetime Chicagoan, stopped his car on another occasion, saying to a stranger, "I know you live in Oak Lawn and some whispering in the atmosphere seems to tell me you need a ride. I have never been in Oak Lawn, though it is only a few miles away, so I would like to take you home and look over the town."

They Split the Cab

Several times cabs have pulled up to the station after other experimenters have said "On," hurried toward the cab, only to find some other person had pre-ordered it. But each time the passenger said, "Come on in and share the cab with me."

The Switch Delivered a Livery Car, Not a Cab

Another account: "Once *I had to have* a cab. None showed. Impatient beyond holding still, I walked east a few blocks to Ashland Ave., a busy corner. Still no cab. Suddenly a black car made a U turn from the other side of the street and pulled up. I saw what resembled a meter in the front seat and queried the driver, 'Is this car a cab?' 'No,' he replied, 'this is a LIVERY CAR, but you look like you need a ride.' He took me home."

Fifteen Seconds to Spare

"I had just a few minutes to make a train in the station in Washington, D.C. There was a snarl of traffic and I made the mistake of having the cab driver let me out a block from the station, thinking I could make better headway on foot. I was caught in the middle of the wide street burdened with a heavy suitcase, with cars rushing at me from all sides.

"Panic seized me and I knew that I was in danger not only of losing my train but my life. So I relaxed and said 'ON.' A big policeman rushed at me, grabbed my suitcase, and shouting orders at me and at traffic, rushed my bag to a waiting red cap a hundred yards ahead. I boarded the train fifteen seconds before it left!"

Is It Telepathy?

Too many incidents have happened not only in Chicago but all over the country, to dispute the power of the switchword "On" when a dire need for transportation presents itself. Several times experimenters temporarily lost faith in the switch and began a walk in the general direction they wanted to go. Before they had walked very far, help would appear.

Now what can we say works this magic? Is it telepathy? Perhaps. Some Good Samaritans have stated they thought of the people they helped before seeing them. And perhaps telepathy works best with anyone who believes in it, and has acquired skill in using the machines in his underground factory. These machines can do anything within the realm of possibility, once they are restored to working order and have been switched on properly.

11

HOW
TO CAST OFF
YOUR BURDENS

The SWITCHWORD TO USE WHEN YOU FACE A BURDENSOME task, not to your conscious liking, is "Adjust."

Several elderly people with heart conditions or burdened with overweight have used it effectively in climbing a necessary flight of stairs. If you do not like stairs and your doctor has warned you not to climb them, or to climb them slowly when you have to, silently say "adjust" as you face the stairs.

Climb the Stairs

Many tests have elicited reports like the following:

Did Not Even Puff

"I said 'adjust' at the foot of a steep flight of stairs going to the 'El.' I went up quite briskly and on reaching the top was not even puffing."

Has a Feeling of Elation

"When I say 'adjust' before going up the stairs, I find myself doing strange things. Sometimes I pause on a certain step and take a deep breath. Sometimes I pause for several moments on the intermediate landing. Sometimes I find myself thinking of a hundred and one other things, and give the stairs no thought at all. I get all the way up without any effort, and in negotiating the stairs, have a feeling of elation."

Natural Prudence

"I was directed to the upper floor of a tall building and told by the elevator starter there was a flight of stairs to climb at the end. I reached these described stairs, said 'adjust' and looking up, found there were *two flights more* than I was told. I turned around and took the elevator back to the ground floor." *Note:* The foregoing is a good example of the natural prudence always found in Perfect Living.

Enjoys Climbing

"When I say 'adjust' in climbing stairs, I now ascend much more slowly than in the past, but not only is my impatience conquered, but I actually seem to enjoy the act of slowly ascending the stairs."

Hire Help?

You are often told to avoid too much work around the house, the lawn, the garden, and especially never to try to shovel much snow in winter. Too much exertion, and especially the exertion of doing distasteful jobs, can cause heart strokes, or bring on a serious state of near-exhaustion.

"Hire some help" is the advice of your well-wishers. This is good advice, too, provided you have the money to pay for the help and if, willing to pay for the help, you find there is help available at a price. But with no money to throw away and no help anywhere in sight, the job still has to be done and you are elected.

Say "adjust" when there is no one to help you lift a heavy object, and you find yourself turning quickly into a master engineer studying out leverage and scientific means of defying gravity. Your sub-self knows how to get the heavy object lifted without straining your body.

Report: "People tell me I do too much work on my lawn in summer and persist in cautioning me about shoveling snow in winter. They do not know that I have learned to *like* such work, because the switchword 'adjust' which turns on the burden-chasing machine inside me gives me a grand feeling of self-togetherness in these tasks.

He Found New Work Tricks

"Staring at one such completed job, I stopped to review exactly what I did in executing the work. I found many unusual things had happened. First, in starting, I had committed myself to doing only a small fraction of the work ahead, an amount which reason said was not too much. Then, as I went along, every quarter hour or so, I would unconsciously abandon the tool or implement with which I had been working, and change to another which was called for by a different phase of the work. The new tool not only gave rest to the muscles involved in one phase, but seemed to restore all the pep and energy expended previously, while giving new interest and verve to the muscles involved in the second phase. By splitting a burdensome, even awesome, job up into small parts requiring various help from many parts of the body, I get a great deal done and am never tired at the end.

"People, much younger and stronger than I, confess they actually HATE cutting a lot of grass, shoveling a lot of snow

They simply have not discovered the wonders of the switchword 'adjust'!"

Comment: If too few parts of your body are "honored" by assigning them to a special job, the other parts are jealous and resentful at being ignored. If the conscious side of you will only ask all of your experience, all of your ability to share in any job, the underside of you immediately shows its gratitude by making ALL of you feel grand.

The Switchword for Subduing Excitement: COVER

"Never run after a streetcar or a woman—there will be another along in a minute," said the old comic postcard. But the streetcars are passing out, and they do not run every minute.

A business executive who has experimented faithfully in his studies of the science of Perfect Living has isolated the switchword to turn on the machine that subdues all unwanted excitement.

On many occasions he has found himself hurrying, even running, to catch his train to the city. He says: "If it's a close call, I HAVE TO RUN, though I know I shouldn't. I also know there won't be another train along in a minute, no, not for an hour."

Of course he should start earlier, but few people do all the things they should do.

This man is not in good physical condition. It used to take him a good half-hour to recover his poise after a short run. Now, he simply tells himself he wants to return to normal immediately, and silently says: "Cover." The excitement, the gasping for breath, the physical turmoil vanish in a minute!

"Cover" is the switch for reducing excitement.

Case History: An argumentative man began to notice that as he entered an argument or a crusade of some kind, his blood pressure shot up alarmingly. Symptoms: sudden nervousness, trembling voice, anger, and a dull walloping pain in the back of his neck.

He was advised to say "Cover" when he noticed himself slipping into the excitement of each argument. He was also advised, after he had slipped, to say "Cover" anyway.

He always loved argument and now he can argue with impunity. He never blows his top if he uses "Cover" in time, but holds up his end with sound logic, calm demeanor, and an even tone in his voice. If he forgets to switch on his excitement-erasing machine in time, and gets excited, he can hurry back to even temper almost immediately with the switchword "Cover."

Case History: A prominent business man was driving himself into becoming a public speaker. On the first few attempts he found his voice trembling, his breath running short, his knees knocking, and an overpowering weakness running through his whole body.

On his next speech, he silently said: "Cover" when he sensed inner excitement over the ordeal to come. He said: "Cover" as he stood up to make the vital speech. It went off well, with all trace of fear and panic removed.

Note: Fear is the most common cause of excitement—fear of missing out, fear of losing your life, fear of being ridiculed or insulted, fear of not being able to muster up your full powers in a given act. If you can honestly confess to fear (some people are too afraid to admit they are afraid) you must then and there admit that you are NOT TOGETHER WITH YOURSELF. Submit to this simple truth, and though fear remains, you feel better at once.

12

MERGING
YOURSELF
INTO "ONENESS"

An HONEST PERSON, READING HIMSELF OUT LOUD, AND
speaking for his conscious self and his subconscious self
at one and the same time, can consistently utter these words:
"I know that I have in me the makings of a single person with
a name that is the same as my name, John Smith. I am not
two John Smiths. This combination of body and soul, known as
John Smith, belongs to me and to me alone. My Conscious Mind
is intended by nature to do my thinking and my willing. My
subconscious self is intended by nature to do my feeling, my
unconscious thinking and willing, to accumulate and store all
experience I get out of life, real or imaginary.

"In nature there is nothing hostile or contradictory about
these two sides of myself. God would not have created me, if it
were not possible for me to live with myself in a perfect merging

of my conscious, surface life and my subconscious, subsurface life.

"In spite of the awful evidence of history that nearly every man who ever lived allows himself to be split up into two enemy camps, to wage a continuing war, mild or violent, on himself, it need not happen in my case. *I am legally and properly only ONE.* Oneness is my Pre-Destiny and my Immediate-Destiny, and the Something Bigger in me, that I have always known was there, the key to Perfect Living is my Self-Togetherness!"

How to Invite Togetherness
Into Your Being

Let us try a few experiments in Self-Togetherness. Maybe, by seeing that the tiniest trace of your own Togetherness can make you happier in a moment, you will acknowledge your right to Perfect Living. Consider:

1. Lovely Contemplations

As you sit there, still holding this book, recall a fresh, blue day in spring or autumn, the mild breeze, the beneficent fairness in the air, or a gentle young girl's face, beaming and smiling and exuding overpowering pleasantness.

Recall the friend you have never met, the stranger who has boosted you, praised you behind your back for no apparent motive other than his own goodness of heart. A food whose delightful memory still overwhelms you—somebody's great chocolate ice cream, Mrs. Jones's wonderful blackberry pie. Does your mouth water over the memory of a delicious meal? Let it. That's the Apartness fading out and the Togetherness coming in!

Bring back to mind a great achievement, the time you came through so grandly in an unforgettable deed. It doesn't matter how long ago it happened, you can still recall the beauty of your performance, the glory you felt in your accomplishment. Perhaps you cannot remember all the details now. That's fine! For if the details are clear, then your conscious side would want to claim all the glory. But if your accomplishment happened many years ago, you are now ready to give the other-than-conscious side its proper share of credit. At least, it is not ignored, not humiliated. Both sides of you deserve equal credit *for you, and only you, did the great thing!* Now—you can feel yourself, see yourself coming together with yourself, getting on your own side. Isn't it lovely?

A Tourist's "Grand View." Years ago, on a wonderful Sunday morning, a visitor was strolling along a hill in an Iowa city, when suddenly he reached a great eminence, and before him rose up a marvelous vista, a sight of the countryside that carried the eye for miles in all directions. He could see farms, forests, distant towns.

"My what a grand view!" he exclaimed. And having said "grand view," he wanted to remember the lovely place and walked over to read a street sign. The sign said "Grand View Boulevard." He can now think of this view, this incident, and feel the oneness, the Togetherness in his soul all over again.

Save all your souveniers of joy and peace. Your memory still holds them; search it freely and bring them back at will. The lapse of the years only make the Oneness, the Togetherness, more rich and precious.

2. *Try Substituting "We" for "I"*

Once in a while you meet a wise and gentle soul, who gives every sign of being more serene than the average man. Listen to him talk. Notice how rarely he uses the word "I." Notice, too, when he is forced to deal with the personal pronoun, how generously he uses the word WE or its variants. "We will get into it." "We tried this once." "We were only twenty years old at the time."

Instinctively he seems to avoid the word "I," not because the

"I" is offensive to his listeners, it is *offensive to himself*. For that word "I" scratches and wounds the subconscious, makes it rear up in resentment. "I" is a totally conscious word, claiming to represent the full personality when, in truth, it represents only a part, and often a very small part.

Substitute "We" for "I" in your speaking. More important still, in your silent inward meditation, drop the "I" entirely and try to standardize on "We," "Us" and "Ours" as the personal pronouns which best represent yourself, your thoughts, feelings, and all your activities, visible or invisible.

This is supreme honor for the "big rascal" in you that resorts to so much pouting, objecting and obstructing, when it is slighted in your deliberations and reckonings. *And it should not be slighted;* it is too important, too necessary to you and your happiness. Honored, it comes to flower, with a dignified might that is near-divine. It loves the "togethering process"; it wants to unite, completely and prodigiously, with the conscious You. It is in a great hurry to cooperate, and to help coordinate your person into an invincible Oneness.

3. Stop Lecturing, Chastising, Blaming

Stop lecturing your own underself, commanding it to do things it doesn't want to do, and blaming it for all the personal errors of your conscious mind, poor judgments, and wrong decisions.

Better still, blame the conscious side for all your troubles, your miseries, your irritations, and faulty living. Surely, your subself is more natural than your conscious. Blame does not belong with the natural side of you, the side which cannot speak out loud, cannot make a single claim for itself, cannot get into communication with the outside world. Your subconscious, subsurface self is what it is, and cannot be held responsible for its acts in the way your free-willing conscious soul is responsible.

This great workhorse inside you should be *thanked* for all the work it does, for its on-the-jobness twenty-four hours a day. There is absolutely nothing the matter with it that a little understanding and sympathy will not cure.

If any blame is coming to you for your deeds, blame your conscious mind, especially for its irrational depreciation of the importance of your subconscious self. When self-administering this blame, do not use the pronoun "We." You have identified your conscious self with "I"—use it now. "I am ignorant." "I am lazy." "I am sloppy." "I am careless." Don't say it out loud—say it to yourself. Your subconscious self will hear, and applaud. It is sweet music to hear the conscious belittling *itself* for a change.

4. *Honor Your Subconscious With Self-Faith*

If your conscious intellect, and all your other mental equipment, could rid you of fear, weakness, uncertainty, you would have been perfect long ago.

You always give your biggest problems to your subsurface self. This is the right thing to do, remembering that when you give the BIG JOB to the subconscious, you should formally release all conscious claim to the work, and to the credit that may accrue to its being completed. Trust that deep down, underside of yourself, the side with all that experience at solving problems, completing onerous tasks, sometimes even doing the "impossible." The more trust you put in your subconscious self, the more confidence you create for your whole self.

5. *The "Alphonse and Gaston" Technique for Producing Togetherness*

Liken your relationship between conscious and subconscious to the two famous characters, Alphonse and Gaston. These two Frenchmen are eternally polite, each always putting himself in the second place, insisting: "After you, my dear Alphonse," and being answered: "No, you come first, my dear Gaston." You will find that when you act magnanimously toward your subconscious self, the Sub-You will jump to outstrip that very magnificence in its show of cooperation with the conscious.

Shake Hands With Your Other Self. Shake hands with yourself, not as with someone you have been fighting, but with a long lost friend. Your subself will respond in kind, with a rush of joy that says: "You, too, are a grand guy!"

Talk about yourself shamelessly, expose your conscious weaknesses publicly, and your frank confessions will not advertise you as weak. Your underself will rush to get meaning into what you say, defending your confessing conscious, and your very humility and openness will come out as pure strength. For the subconscious self, knowing far more about self than the conscious, will not allow its conscious brother to harm himself in the eyes of the world.

How Alphonse Talks to Gaston. Conscious Alphonse says to subconscious Gaston: "Do you feel like going on a reducing diet?" Gaston replies: "After you, my dear Alphonse!" But Alphonse persists: "You come first, my dear Gaston. I refuse to declare this diet into existence unless it is completely agreeable to you!" Momentarily Gaston is nonplussed. He does not feel like a rigid diet right now. He would prefer to keep on eating, getting fatter and fatter; he likes the wildness of gluttony, the outlawry of surfeit. But, above all, he is polite. "My dear Alphonse," he murmurs, "I love you more than anything else in the world, even more than food. Tell me, do you believe we both need this diet?" And conscious Alphonse now says to subconscious Gaston: "Dear friend, dear alter ego, I feel we do, but will undertake nothing of the kind unless you accompany me through all the denial and discipline involved."

They seesaw back and forth, drowning each other with politeness, deferring and submitting to each other, till finally, Gaston who has the last say, declares: "Alphonse, my conscious Alphonse, I really love this proposed discipline almost as much as I love you. Now that we each know the other wants it, *let us get to it!*"

If you have ever gone on a major diet (successful) or a crusade of self-reform, such as an abstention from all drinking, smoking, candy-eating, or something else you were overdoing, was not the project prefaced with a similar excessively polite conversation with yourself?

Creating a Heaven of Anticipation. Again, Alphonse says to Gaston: "Dear Gaston, I have purchased *for you* a new suit of clothes, very stylish, a beautiful hat, and an expensive pair of shoes!" "For me?" asks Gaston in astonishment. "Yes, for you, dear friend, entirely for you! Gaston, these fashionable things will be delivered tomorrow." Subconscious Gaston is flattered, and spends this whole day in a heaven of *anticipation.* Oh, if your subconscious can only get into the habit of *anticipating* good things to come, benefits and benisons devised and created by your gracious, conscious self, how happy it will be!

In the cartoon, Alphonse and Gaston are always *together.* The inspired cartoonist hardly ever needed to draw in strangers or things or foreign events to keep the action delectable and joyous. The two polite characters were enough, all by themselves, to make the beautiful story of mutual agreement born of extravagant politeness. And to the observer, Alphonse and Gaston, were actually not two different men, but a *single character,* made miraculously delightful by their flawless and eternal deference to each other.

6. *"To Each His Own"*

All internal fighting comes from thoughtless, ignorant trespassing on one side of you by the other side.

To your subconscious subsurface soul, you leave natural activities like digestion, growth, healing, breathing, blood circulation.

Then, contradicting, you suddenly turn around and rob it of pride, glory.

From it you demand obedience, sometimes abject humiliation and subservience.

It can do a staggering amount of work, but long before its endurance can show itself, your conscious side announces: "I am tired."

It can work with stupefying speed, but your conscious insists: "I cannot go that fast."

Your subconscious soul is quite willing to forget and forgive an insult or a wound received from the outside. But your conscious pride says: "I will never forgive that fellow. Revenge is mine."

Your subself loves to improvise, ad lib, create on the spot. Your conscious interferes with: "I am not prepared to make a fool of myself."

Invite Your Subconscious
Into Your Plans

How easy it would be for all of us to get together with ourselves, to step into a new life of unmitigated bliss, if we would let each part of us do the work ordained for it by nature.

Your conscious is always telling yourself: "I can't do a darn thing. I'm not mechanical. I'm no good at figures. I'm good for nothing." Your subconscious self is insulted and angered by such foolish talking, representing itself as the whole of you. It knows: "Together we can do anything, no objective too difficult, no task too stupendous." For in the vast uncharted regions of your personal underground self, you hold and remember every experience in which you ever figured, an infinitude of wisdom, skill and power.

Your conscious seems to want to stay apart, to live in the Apartness which is misery and unrest and incompletion of the person. Your underself wants to get together with the conscious side of you, wants to do great deeds, achieve miraculous accomplishments. Why not invite it into your plans, into your life?

Each side of you has its own proper job. Your conscious can

have the words, provided they are the right words. Your subconscious self wants to go to work, wants to coordinate its might with your conscious intellect and will, wants to see a happy union take place, the marriage of your two selves into a single, glorious, *happy person.*

13

A WORD
CAN SAVE YOUR LIFE

Almost EVERYONE ENJOYS, NOW AND THEN, A TEMPO-
rary share of Self-Togetherness, and feels this thing we
loosely refer to as happiness. If you win a raffle, or your
stocks go up, or you make a lucky shot in golf, if the local ball
club has a fine winning streak, you feel great each time your mind
turns to dwell on the favorable event.

Let us examine the anatomy of some of these temporary
flashes. Some baseball fans are such rabid rooters that they regularly go to bed with a "broken heart" when the home team loses,
and with a "seventh heaven of delightful feeling" after it wins.

Now just what has the fan done to help his team win? He is
not a player. He cannot make a hit. He cannot strike out an opponent. He must sit far away from the ball diamond if at the
park, and miles away if he is listening to the game on TV or radio.
He can root, yes; but the actual ball players, nearly always
strangers to him, play the actual game. But the team wins and the
fan elates. Why? Whence this single flash of Perfect Living?

How a Rooter Gets Together With Himself

As a person the fan has, as usual, his two opposite warring camps, his conscious mind which tells the world he is a rooter for such and such a team, and his much bigger subconscious and subterranean self (which knows more about baseball than his conscious side could ever recite) and which in this case should be opposed to all this useless rooting.

There is no money to be made in being a rooter, no fame or success; distraction and recreation, perhaps, but no profit.

There may be cheering and shouting in it for the conscious side of this man, and even that small satisfaction of the conscious self should arouse the opposition of the subconscious. But, strangely, it does not. Actually both sides of the true rooter *get together in this rooting,* get together in the genuine joy of victory if the team wins.

"What Is There in It for Us?"

But the fan's subterranean self is experienced and practically all-knowing; it is also sly and cunning, and intensely vigilant in observing all the machinations of the conscious side. As the subterranean self observes the visible and audible effects of the conscious rooting, it inquires: "What is there in it for him and what is there in it for me?"

Seeing no chance of the conscious obtaining credit for helping his team win, the fan subconsciously reflects: "If the team does win he cannot say *he* made it win, that *he* caused the victory. If the team loses, I, in all fairness cannot blame him for making the team lose, so I believe I will go over to his side. After all, I always want to get together with him, but cannot stand his gloating and strutting where there is a chance for his stealing credit for the things I do. In this case, I do nothing; he does nothing, so let's root together."

The sub-fan enjoys seeing the visible fan root for an outcome neither fan can affect. Here the conscious side of the fan is forced by circumstances to engage in an activity that is basically foolish because it contains no chance for ability or effectiveness. The subterranean side is not really rooting, but only getting together with the conscious side because the conscious is here making a fool of itself in terms of so-called rational efficiency. But the feeling of Self-Togetherness is definitely real even before the game is won or lost. The two sides are together, and if victory happens, *they rejoice together*. And this transitory joy is definitely the result of an artificially made self-union.

Gloom in Defeat

If, instead of victory, defeat happens, real gloom pervades the fan; now his underself, supremely intelligent in its silent way, begins to berate the conscious self, which claims all the intelligence of the person, for its stupidity in engaging in an effort over which neither side had any control. Thus the Self-Togetherness is shattered, and the inner war again rages.

Could Not Reduce an Ounce More Than 900 Pounds

Let us look at the case of the man, endowed with a big-boned body who early in life saw, and immediately acknowledged, that he was inclined to a sloppy obesity, probably the result of a low metabolism. An enormous eater, as he grew older his appetite seemed to increase with age and his weight zoomed to record-breaking heights.

Through the years, while still fairly young, he had gone on perhaps three or four crash reducing diets every year. He found he could take off ten pounds in a week, fifteen in two weeks and fifty pounds in three months.

Time went on, and his eating went on, and then as he reached and passed middle age, he discovered that his body could neither stand a crash diet nor his will power sustain one. His will power failed and his body resisted, not because the doctors advised against quick reducing at his age but because his real subconscious self put down its iron hand in resisting.

Now past sixty and weighing 250 pounds (when he should weigh less than 200), he fell into a mood of despondency. He had taken off more than *900 pounds* by diets in his earlier years and now he could not reduce a pound.

Then he heard a little about Perfect Living. He came up with a new idea. He said to himself: "I still have will power. I have gone on the water wagon for a year at a time, many times, because I love to drink as much as I love to eat and it is still easy for me to abstain from alcoholic drink a year at a time. Suppose I now go on a slow reducing diet for ONE WHOLE YEAR, as if I were on the water wagon, and see what happens." He tried it. It worked for about six months and he did take off some twenty-five pounds. Then his new slow reducing diet began to slip and, though he was feeling much better, much younger, and happier with this new accomplishment, all of his old weight gradually came back.

But failure of the Perfect Living system should never disturb its advocate. The Perfect Living person knows that HE MUST KNOW HIMSELF, MUST KEEP ON LEARNING HOW TO KNOW HIMSELF, until he achieves perfection at the art.

He Substitutes the Will to Live

Our fat man, old and sick, and carrying the terrible burden of fifty pounds of excess weight, meditated further. "I have will power," he said to himself, "though I have seemed to lose it in the reducing realm. But I know I still have it. My mistake has been in believing that all my will power comes from my conscious mind, which is indeed the smallest part of me! My subconscious, my immense underself with its unlimited experience, has enormously more power than my conscious mind. I must get together with myself on this matter of taking off weight, I must get on MY OWN SIDE."

This time, aided by his increased insight into Perfect Living, he seized upon a richer "together" type of objective, *the will to live*. His surface self addressed his underself! "Both of us will die in a few short years, if we do not take off the weight—right?" "Agreed," answered his underself. "Now both of us have one thing in common, don't we, and that is the *will to live*—right?" "Absolutely right," replied his real BIG self, "other men live to be eighty, ninety, a hundred, and stay healthy till the end. We both WANT to do that, don't we?" "Yes, yes," said his conscious mind, "and if you'll agree to do most of the work, for you are invincible once you tackle a tough objective, I will cooperate in every way my own nature will permit."

After twelve months, that fat old man now weighs 200 pounds and looks ten years younger. When asked for his secret of taking off excess weight so healthfully and successfully, he replies: "'We,' meaning 'myself' and 'I,' did not go on a diet at all. After an honest meeting and discussion with each other, we simply adopted a sensible objective—to live a long and healthy life."

Your Objective Must Be Selfish

An examination of this case history reveals many salient points in the system of Perfect Living.

You must have an objective. It must be a selfish one. It must be difficult of achievement. It must appeal to and win the sustained approval of both sides of you. You must be capable (and here is where the conscious mind enters with full importance) of announcing this objective out loud and in plain English, and repeat it frequently to yourself.

The objective of living a long and healthy life will carry many small, sub-objectives with it. In the fat man's case the objective, supported by his two sides, not only took off fifty pounds for him in a single year but in the meantime gave him a marvelous balance between his subconscious and his conscious mind.

At one point in his diet he was asked what word-switch he used to help him cut down on his eating. Reflection caused him to announce that in this case his long-term but prime objective—long life—worked like a word-switch when he was being tempted by a wolfish appetite and appealing foods.

He simply repeated his objective, which instantly consolidated his Self-Togetherness, constantly nourished by the natural will to live!

One normally should eat food to live, but it is all too true that "We dig our graves with our teeth." However, the above warning deters very few from overeating, because it is an appeal to reason.

But the will to live rages strongly in the subconscious, undoubtedly more strongly than in the conscious mind. The sub-you will not easily relinquish it. The conscious now has no quarrel whatever with it. Both sides of you like the objective, truly *want* the objective and thus invincible Self-Togetherness is engendered.

The Big Accomplishment
Brings Other Victories With It

Our friend the fat man found out that the weeks or months needed in the accomplishing of a tough objective are freighted with unspeakable joy, release from tension. And the accomplishment of a score of other goals which are not stated in the original objective are easy to reach when any person gets on his own side.

This is why the master switch to the whole subterranean factory sometimes works magic long before the principles of Perfect Living are formally learned. If the newcomer has a transient flash of Self-Togetherness due to a fine rest, a streak of luck, he unknowingly falls into the proper "Together" mood. While still in this mood, he says "Together" as a real word switch as he confronts a special objective, and thus strengthens the accidental "Together" mood already pervading his person.

Exploiting the Flash

Just as a proper arousal and sustaining of the natural will to live, with its full-hearted endorsement by both sides of the individual, scientifically produces a definite Self-Togetherness, so also accidental or temporary Self-Togetherness can be exploited on many an occasion by throwing on the master switch to your whole subterranean factory.

One incipient disciple, a poor bowler, tried the system with "Together" as a switch and turned in a phenomenal (for him) series. Investigation revealed that he had received a raise in pay that same day and was feeling good, bowling or no bowling. The raise in pay was a tribute to his subconscious experience and ability as well as to his conscious self. Both parts of him were firmly together because they were getting proper credit for the good fortune that had come to him.

It Can Save Your Life in a Second

"Together" will not always deliver on minor objectives, but certainly helps on major ones.

If you have ever been close to death in a near-miss automobile collision, and if the accident was prevented by your quick reflexes and skill, you knew you had a major objective here (to save your life while it was in immediate danger). You also had the feeling that ALL OF YOU, not merely your planning or seeing side, but all of you and the experiences of many self-prevented accidents and near-misses in your past, suddenly surged into your single soul. Instant Self-Togetherness, created by a major and im-

mediate need, saved your life where all the intelligence in the
world could not.

A Natural Right

The transitory flashes of Self-Togetherness, constantly occurring in all human beings, certainly prove that there is such a
thing as self-union, that such union is potent beyond description
and the finest embodiment of "happiness" man can at present
envision. It does not last for long, but something deep inside of
all of us keeps prompting: "It should be possible to make it last
forever."

Regardless of whatever beliefs you hold about the life here-
after, it is your right, yes, your duty, to believe there is such a
thing as HEAVEN ON EARTH, uninterrupted by gloom, failure
or evil of any kind. The joy of Self-Togetherness is so sublime, so
ineffable, that from the little bit you have seen of it in temporary
flashes, it seems that its permanent possession should be your
natural right.

14

HOW
TO END
"APARTNESS"

When YOU "BLOW YOUR TOP" IN A NERVOUS OUT-
burst, or fly off the handle in uncontrolled anger, you don't
feel healthier; you *are sicker*. Any emotional flurry that
causes you to come apart at the seams is a real setback.

And when there is no visible crisis of any kind, such as pain,
illness, loss of fear, in your so-called "normal" state, *you may
still feel punk*. You need not be a victim of melancholy or depres-
sion, you can be absolutely normal and still be far from peace and
joy. Worrisome reminders and negative suggestions are all around
you. You seem to be a vast receptacle for sorrow and sadness,
some of it your own, some of it the unwelcome gift of nearly
every person you meet. And, of course, you always need more
money.

Are We All Doomed to "Apartness"?

Let's not call this non-joyous state "sorrow." It is too normal, too universal, to suggest suffering. In the vicissitudes of life, we nearly all "get by," but few of us are happy even part of the time. We are not exactly sad, either, though we are always mildly conscious of internal unrest and disquietude.

Is There a Screw Loose Somewhere?

This condition of personality is called Apartness. When another person flies into a violent rage, we all recognize Apartness in its magnification. Mania, lunacy, insanity are exaggerated evidences of Apartness. Of a slightly balmy person, we say: "There's a screw loose somewhere"—suggesting he's coming apart. Yes, it is easy to recognize Apartness in the extreme.

But we are very reluctant to confess that Apartness has any tenancy in our own selves.

We have seen that many acts of pure submission tend to guide us toward personal peace and exaltation.

Now, when you submit to Something Bigger, don't you also get a *mended feeling?* As if something inside you had been cracked and now suddenly is *fixed?* Don't you feel the rush of new health and fresh self-satisfaction? Something must have been wrong for its leaving to produce this remarkable peace. Apartness existed within you, perhaps in only a mild form, but it did hold distress with it. Then, thank goodness, the separated parts of your complete self were rejoined in an act of pure submission. At once, joy stepped in, took over to uplift your person.

But not for long.

Are You "All in One Piece"?

A twinge of envy and, poof! Apartness comes back and joy escapes. You see a stranger's face; you do not like it; something inside you is chipped. A bit of heedless criticism is directed at you, or directed by you at another, and—there's that bugaboo Apartness again.

Apartness is no joke. It is a universal scourge. If it were not for Apartness, we would all be back in the Garden of Eden, living the glorified life in glorified bodies, knowing nothing about pain, misery, fear or insecurity.

We all know we are not as happy as we would like to be, nor as happy as we believe WE COULD BE and SHOULD BE. We all keep on lacking things we want, wanting things we cannot get, and wanting to lose certain miseries we cannot shake. Yes, we are cracked, too; not nearly so badly as the lunatic, but still marred by millions of little fissures and wrinkles that destroy the smoothness of a perfect personality.

We are not "all in one piece."

Is This "Life"?

Very few of us are psychopathic cases, very few of us are mentally sick. But who of us is rash enough to declare he is in perfect mental health?

Who of us is entirely free of

Pain
Worry
Fear
Hypersensitiveness
Self-torment
Irritability
Eagerness to fight, to argue, to make trouble
Reluctance to fight
Evasion of duty
Unexplained low spirits
Procrastination

Laziness
Remorse
Complaining
Nervousness
Temper
Indecision
Forgetting
Addiction to making mistakes

and a hundred other human failings that keep perfect peace out of our hearts? The forms of Apartness are almost too numerous to list. Too readily we concede them to be necessary elements of human nature. "That's life!" we say, and let it go at that. But are all these hideous and distressing elements indispensable? Are we all forever doomed to Apartness?

Some Causes of Apartness

Some of it is inherited or picked up in family environment as you grow up from babyhood.

Some of it is copied from other people, for nearly everyone you meet or know shows signs of distress of some kind. Certainly perpetual mental poise is not the style; in fact if anyone shows signs of being happy for too long a period of time, we get suspicious of him.

Some Apartness is definitely caused by the newspapers, magazines, movies and communication media, with stories of fire, danger, crime, outlawry and delinquency of every kind. Even the so-called "funnies" are constituted for the most part of crime, abuse and disaster.

Some of this Apartness just happens to you accidentally. You "catch" a cold you never wanted; you slip and fall, or a cinder blows in your eye.

Some of it comes to you under the simple law of averages; you lose money, you suffer a setback, you find your hair getting gray or falling out, or you realize your age when you notice the many things people younger than you can do, but which are now beyond your capacity.

Apartness enters your personality in myriad ways over which you seem to have no control. But the most vicious kind of Apartness, and in the heaviest volume, is the Apartness you make for yourself.

He Tried to Ruin His Own Instep

There is the case of the patient who complained to his doctor of an agonizing pain in his instep on awakening every morning. The doctor X-rayed the foot, could find no broken bones or bruises. The patient could not even confess to the pain when in the doctor's presence, for it only lasted about an hour, first thing in the morning. Now the doctor knew this man too well to attribute the pain to his imagination; the patient was reliable, emotionally stable, and very well educated.

Both agreed the pain was real and *something was causing it*. After much deliberation the doctor gave his diagnosis: "You are causing this pain in your own instep by something you are doing to yourself in the night."

The patient began to study himself as he arranged his legs for sleeping, and accidentally caught himself using the heel of one foot to press sharply down on the instep of the other. He was probably doing it all night long in his sleep, for his dreams had been painful too. Then, being a broad-minded person, he had to acknowledge the awful truth: *he was inflicting this terrible pain on himself for no good reason!*

For when he rearranged his feet and bed clothes so that the offending heel couldn't get at the instep in the night, his trouble vanished promptly and for good!

The Apartness We Make for Ourselves

This is the kind of Apartness which we make for ourselves! It seems that we all unconsciously seek an overshare of clean-cut misery. You have just had a wonderful dinner; it leaves a fine taste in your mouth—so you hurry to light a cigar or cigarette to drive the fine feeling away.

It is a lovely day. You feel wonderful, as you step out on your way to work. But suddenly you see the face of a person you do not like. Instantly you rush into a turmoil of silent criticism of that person, memory of all his faults and doings, and your perfect day is lost in a second. For a moment you were together with yourself and in the throes of flawless feeling; now you are APART *and you feel terrible!*

The Barbers Agree

Joe, the barber, struggling with an agonizing pain in the sacroiliac and still trying to work at his trade, says: "I ask you, why should I drop my comb five times as often with this terrible back pain as I do when things are normal?" He gets the answer, "Believe it or not, you're not in enough pain with your bad back, you must want still more pain."

A barber of olden time, who had shaved thousands of customers in his day reports: "Most of them complained that the razor was not sharp, I was hurting them. But with a safety razor there can be just as much pain as with an open blade. The difference is: when a person is inflicting pain on himself, he can stand an unlimited amount, without having enough sense to know he is doing it!"

The Constant Attack on Self

Life is a constant attack on self. Thousands, yea hundreds of thousands, of adults still bite their fingernails to the bone, unable to stop the "habit."

The so-called "unintentional" mistake is really no accidental mistake at all but a deliberate attempt by the unseen, unrecognized side of you to prove that your conscious side is not so perfect after all.

You find yourself driving along peacefully in your car, when suddenly you are behind a fellow motorist you are sure is a stupid driver. Then you start hoping he will stop suddenly, make an unwarranted turn or without warning move out of his channel, all to prove (to yourself)that he is a "stupid driver." Certainly you are now in distress. Certainly you have inflicted this distress on yourself. For whether your opinion of that driver is justified or not, you can do nothing about his driving, except perhaps drive fast and pass him up. If you do decide to pass him, you may also decide to pause in passing and shout a loud: "Wake up, you dope!" into his open window, or at least give him a dirty look.

Does detecting his mistakes or shouting at him make you feel any better? Not a bit. You feel worse: you have inflicted more pain on yourself.

"Adjust" Prevented Her From Ruining Her Ankle

A housewife sprained her ankle slightly, with moderate pain and swelling resulting. But that was not enough. Later the same day she sharply bumped the ankle against a chair leg, and again a table leg. The swelling increased. She tried to be careful. Next morning she opened the refrigerator door and a heavy can of fruit dropped on the same sore foot. "It may become a habit," she mused, "I better use that switch 'Adjust'." She did and her ankle trouble was soon over.

The Dentist Had "Dropsy"

The dentist was constantly dropping things—his materials, his tools, any objects he picked up. It looked very unprofessional to his patients and the dentist knew it. When he finally realized that his dropping troubles were not due to nervousness but that for some unknown reason *he was making himself drop things,* he silently said "Uncle" (*a plea for mercy from his subsurface self*), and the bad habit vanished.

Amateur typists make some queer mistakes on the typewriter. Sometimes a combination of these mistakes makes a cryptic message that is startling. Equally appalling is the multitude of daily mistakes we all make in speaking, spelling, acting, forgetting.

The human knack for "looking for trouble," and inevitably finding it, caused the old-time oriental philosopher to give off this bit of worldly wisdom: "See no evil, hear no evil, speak no evil." We talk against people behind their backs trying to prove how smart we are, but there is no joy in it. Even when we plan to hurt someone or think about it without going through with the plan, we heap distress upon ourselves.

All Egomaniacs in a Degree

We regard the egomaniac, the person who is always thinking of himself and talking about himself as a rare species. Yet we are all egomaniacs in one degree or another. The person who always has a chip on his shoulder, the incessant arguer and contradicter, the pouter who fights by not saying a single word, are all egomaniacs. In all cases of egomania we see the rank Apartness of these two personal "souls" Goethe refers to as the war raging inside the individual.

The Material Comes From Life

It is true that life itself presents nearly all the material, real or imaginary, which starts the war inside. Examine a few familiar distresses and if they are not your own, you laugh at any other person who harbors them.

One experimenter writes: "I'm in such bad shape I find myself, while walking in the shopping district, staring into people's faces and making myself feel sick because I see so few faces I like." This man is suffering from a special form of the universal distress of *fear;* he is afraid of strangers! The switch to end this fear—"Cancel."

Another states: "People's faces never distress me, but I am afraid of being seen taking a suit back to the department store where I bought it, because people will see me with the package and know I have made a mistake." This is fear of people's opinions. The protective switch—"Bluff."

From another: "A certain game is my favorite and normally I play very well, but when I get into a crucial contest with a tough competitor, I not only tighten up but my game goes to pieces!" This is the crazy fear of being killed—buck fever. The good switchword here is—"Be."

Everything Happens to Me

Reason tells us that the majority of instances of such silly fears should have no place in our being, yet the sillier the fear and the more unwarranted, the more it distresses us. Real and justified fear such as falling off a high ledge or walking into fire is quickly dealt with by all sane people—they walk or run away from the danger at once.

Fear of fate is expressed in this report: "I make a bet and I know I'll lose. Everything happens to me. I fail in important projects. I get more than my share of flat tires. I never get the breaks—I'm the unluckiest guy in the world." This is the defeatist attitude which so many people have, a bitter distress they carry with them forever, worrying, fearing, failing.

Perfect Living holds out complete hope for all who suffer from fear in its multitude of forms. There is fear-dispelling machinery inside you, and the main switchword that turns it on is—"Bluff!"

But you must realize that this fear-dispeller is the most unused machine in your underground factory. You have not only neglected to use it, you have so abused it and knocked it out of shape with all your useless fears that it will take much time and attention to restore it to working order.

15

HEALING
THE SIX BIG RIFTS

Can YOU REMEMBER THE MANY OCCASIONS, WHEN UN-
explainedly you suddenly felt brave, confident, carefree?
Your joy was so great, you were giddy with joy. Then in an
instant you brought up some fear, some negative consideration,
some thought of cost or loss, and your moment of perfection was
GONE! Here you were gifted with a rare period of bliss. What
spoiled it, who spoiled it? YOU DID. You—only *you*—brought in
the negative thought that ruined your own joy. You made this
Apartness, and you need not have made it!

Are There Two "You's"?

Certainly there are two "you's"! Though they both belong to
the single you, the dignified capable person that sanity insists is
but one individual, there are definitely two sides of you that are
seemingly condemned to wage perpetual war on each other.

Consciously and rationally, you would like to feel good all the time. That is the conscious you speaking. Subconsciously, unconsciously, and most often inexplicably, you are doing things to yourself to make you feel bad. That is the sub-you, the subconscious you, the side of you that is generally called irrational. Since the label "irrational" is easily put on subconscious acts, you can tell yourself you are not really guilty of wanting bad feeling more than good feeling. You know you are a rational man, you know you are sane.

But it is a great mistake to call the subconscious self irrational. The subconscious self is seldom irrational. In so many ways it is more important than your conscious mind; it is your exclusive property; it belongs to no one else, and if you insist consciously that you are rational, then, to be consistent, you must also insist that that very important part of you, your subconscious, is just as rational, as sane and sensible, as your conscious mind!

Insist from the very beginning that your subconscious soul, no matter how awful its actions and how seemingly malevolent its ways, is just as rational as the conscious you, and *perhaps far more rational*.

THE SIX BIG RIFTS

In the treatment your conscious mind gives to your subconscious, you might like to confess that your conscious side is *much more irrational, foolish, juvenile!*

1. The Rift in Size

Let's see what substantiation there may be for this theory:

There is a great division between the subconscious self and the conscious mind in size, importance, experience, work, ability, power. The subconscious self dwarfs the conscious by comparison. Yet, that silly side of you, that "rational" conscious mind, completely ignores the importance of the Great Doer, the subconscious sub-soul, and arbitrarily assumes the role of Declarer,

Caller of the Shots, Master of the Ego. You say: "I am going to do something." When you use the pronoun "I" you definitely mean the conscious you is going to do it. But the principal Doer is not your conscious side but rather your subconscious side. Is it any wonder that the real you balks?

2. *The Rift in Credit*

There's a great division in CREDIT. Your conscious mind is amazingly adept at grabbing *all the credit for every good thing you do.* The subsurface soul naturally wants its proper share of credit, but seldom gets any. In your subconscious system lies all capacity for *feeling*. Credit or honor are things that are *felt*. But your conscious mind has *no power for feeling;* you can *think* with your conscious, you can *will* with your conscious, but you simply cannot *feel* with your conscious. Yet that conscious side of you always insists that all credit for any good work or performance belongs to it. The subconscious you is thus slurred, dishonored—and how can you blame it for acting up and wanting to puncture the blown-up toad that is claiming such undeserved credit?

3. *The Rift in Blame*

There is a great division in BLAME. When something goes wrong, your subconscious self gets all the blame. You as a person know you are being hit with something bad; but your nimble conscious mind can easily "rationalize" its position and prove to you that it is not to blame. But the blame is there nonetheless.

4. *The Rift in Nature*

There is a great division in *nature*. Your conscious is always in touch with the outside world, from whence comes praise and blame, advance or setback, good news or bad news. Your subconscious soul cannot openly reach the outside world, cannot directly be seen or heard by anyone outside of you. It is trapped inside the jail of your person, it has no tongue, no transmitter understandable by any part of the world except yourself.

5. *The Rift in Words*

Your conscious self deals in words, words, words! Sometimes the words compose decisions which you insist are your decisions. But if the decision is not the decision of your TWO "YOU's," your subconscious self will do its best to cancel or nullify the decision.

6. *The Rift in Hearing*

Your subconscious soul hears every word you speak or think. Your conscious you is almost impotent to report with full truth and absolute clarity your countless and complicated subsurface feelings. So your subconscious soul is All-Hearing with respect to what the Real You is doing or thinking, whereas your conscious is almost All-Deaf.

The Mystery of the Dual Nature

Should any of us wonder then, why our two sides are in bitter conflict most of the time? The real mystery is that these two frightening monsters are able to exist at all in the same person. This is the mystery of human nature; this is the explanation, too, of the universal state of non-joy that seems to rule mankind. The wars of gun and powder may start and stop, but the war inside the person goes on forever.

Yet it need not be so! There isn't a man alive who does not know what heaven is. For at some time he has had his moments of heaven on earth in short bursts of joy, in the relief of a heavy burden; in the peace that came mysteriously in the perfume of a wayward zephyr, the miracle of a beautiful face, the sacrifice of a holy love, or a hundred other heavenly, delicious ways. However brief the term of joy, it was proof that human feelings CAN BE PERFECT, that the BEST STATE MAN CAN IMAGINE FOR HIMSELF CAN ACTUALLY BE ENJOYED.

Merely the Beginning of Perfect Living

The real need is not merely to acknowledge that perfect life is possible for all of us on earth, but rather to find out how to achieve an unending and uninterrupted continuance of such perfection.

Undoubtedly, the best way to start is to admit this:

> The ordinary treatment your own conscious mind gives to your subconscious self is cruel, impolite, foolish and *irrational*. If the relations of your conscious side to your subconscious side were *rational*, you would admit it holds most of your power and ability and would give it commensurate honor and credit for all your accomplishments. You would never blame it for your troubles or failures. You would try to read its wishes, try to understand its nature, and always employ it with the reigning attitude of complete trust and cooperation!

The Two "You's" Are Put There to Work Together

The two "you's" that make the single you are put there to work together. The appearance of the slightest trace of Apartness in your personality is flagrant notification that your two parts, rather than working together, are now pulling in opposite directions. The subsurface you has had many years of insult, pushing around, and silly lecturing and sermonizing from your conscious you, and the piled-up resentment it bears towards your decisions and resolutions is shown in the stumbling blocks it presents as soon as you consciously start on a crusade for your so-called "own good."

That subconscious you is powerful!

It can make a million dollars.

It can smoke twenty cigars a day.

It can work a month without sleep.

It can stop you from doing even five minutes of concentrated work.

It can make you seriously sick.

It can cure you of illness doctors might call incurable.

It can actually kill you.

It can save your life.

Properly used and understood, that subsurface you can work any miracle in the realm of the possible.

Both Sides Stymied

But the one thing the sub-you cannot do all by itself is bring you the peace and joy of Perfect Living.

Though your conscious mind may be developed to a state of purest brilliance and be able to do ANYTHING in its own proper realm, *the one thing your conscious mind can never do all by itself is bring you the peace and joy of Perfect Living.*

But there must be an answer. We have had those brief flashes of perfect joy, freedom from all Apartness, invulnerability to temper and fear. Whence comes this joy, so perfect for such a short while? It comes to us and it seems to come *from* us—it *is* us! It is recognized and acclaimed not by one of our two "You's" but by both "you's" in exactly the same way.

It is delivered by your conscious you and the subconscious you *working together with a magic oneness that says there are no longer two "you's,"* two saboteurs of each other's plans—no, in that sacred moment of pure happiness YOU ARE NOW ONE PERSON possessed of a new super-consciousness that rides above and beyond all fear, all pain, all distress, all APARTNESS of any kind.

Exit Apartness—Enter: Self-Togetherness

With Apartness gone, you are now possessed of a new and mighty quality—*Self-Togetherness*.

If all Apartness could be removed from your personality, and blocked forever from reentering, you would be ever after a "Together Person," impervious to disappointment, discouragement, or any condition which could be termed "unhappy." If pain or loss came to you, it would not be an interrupter of your new happiness, for, as you faced it, you would know you had the proper means for managing it perfectly, and naturally.

16

HOW
TO CONQUER
YOUR BASIC FEARS

Four BASIC FEARS EXIST: FEARS OF PEOPLE, FEARS OF *yourself, Fears of Time, and Fears of Fear.* This chapter gives you the switchwords for combating these fears.

1. FEARS OF PEOPLE

Fault-finding

Finding fault with others, developing skill at discovering weakness and inconsistency in others, will begin to eat into your own peace of mind. If you keep it up forever, it will eventually rob you of all the joys of life. Oil up the machine that drives fault-finding out of your mind; turn it on with the switch: PRAISE. And today's awful enemy may be tomorrow's best friend.

Looking for Trouble

Are you looking for a fight, for material for complaining, for anything and everything that may nourish your crabbiness? You will find it right in front of your eyes and all it will do is make you feel bad when you find it. The switchword that works the machine which banishes this weakness is: SHUT. Do not "burn up" when you see an unattended fire in the alley; rather try to recall the last time you yourself started one just like it.

Grudge-Keeping

Keeping a feud alive or holding on to a grudge is supremely foolish. Perhaps it once had some justification; but it delivered a nice "juicy" enemy who is constantly entering your mental house of peace and wrecking it. The burden of any grudge is not easy to relinquish. There is a machine in Perfect Living for destroying old grudges. Its switch is named: REVERSE.

Revenge

The act of revenge is never sweet, always soul-disturbing. If you have ever gone through with an act of revenge you know this. But, worse still, the mere plotting of revenge, or deliberating on whether you should or should not engage in the revenge, may be even more upsetting. It hurts to want to hurt.

Get revenge out of your system by relying on the machine that knows how to chase it out. The switch is: OFF.

Disagreeableness

It takes a lot of hard work to be, and to keep on being, disagreeable. It takes no work at all to be agreeable with people. Flip on this machine with the word-switch: SMILE. Never let an old companion say to you: "Have you forgotten how to smile?"

Arguing and Contradicting

These traits involve perhaps more work than merely being disagreeable. Deceiving with the promise of self-satisfaction, they call for an immense expenditure of mental energy. The switch-word that activates the machine that blocks these tendencies is: CONCEDE. When the motorist said to the traffic cop, "You're right and I'm wrong," the astonished cop replied: "I ought to give you a medal instead of a ticket."

Unfairness and Dishonesty

In indulging in these weaknesses, you dissipate all regard for yourself. Though you know every minute of it is bad, bad, bad, you certify that the war inside your heart is justified. The temptation to steal is in itself enough notification that something has gone wrong with your inner works.

The machine that restores fairness and honesty is switched on with: RESTORE.

Inability to Solve Problems

Problems! All life is full of them, but they need not be definite distresses. The answer-finding machine is operated by the switch: REACH. Often this machine delivers the answer immediately, if a quick answer is needed. Sometimes it waits till morning. Sometimes it works more slowly with complicated problems. Give it time.

Fear of Ridicule

This weakness blocks many a man from attaining worthwhile goals. He is afraid of that unseen, non-existent body: "They say." If "They say" actually existed, the world would have no leaders, no humorists. The machine for creating imperviousness to ridicule is switched on with the word: BE.

Anger

Anger is physically weakening and sometimes delivers a shock to the nervous system that lasts for days. Better watch your blood pressure. Switchword antidote: CLEAR.

Uncertainty and Indecision

The majority of people suffer from these two distresses of the ego. Your conscious mind, much as it loves to brag to your inner self about how brave and competent it is, cannot fool anybody when it comes to making big decisions promptly. Getting the opinions of everyone under the sun does not help either. As the conscious side of you hesitates and fumbles, the big you of your subconscious inner self stubbornly refuses to help. This inner self knows the right decision, but so long as you refuse to consult it or honor it, absolutely NOTHING comes out of it.

Procedure:

FIRST: Submit to Something Bigger—Perfect Living.
SECOND: Say silently: "We want to get rid of this uncertainty."
THIRD: Turn on the switch that puts the uncertainty-removal machine to work. The word is: HELP.

2. FEARS OF YOURSELF

In psychosomatic medicine the specialists stress the fact that the mind may have more to do with the body being sick than the body itself. But a sick or injured body is still your body, is still *you*. In some way, with or without your complete endorsement, it brought this sickness or injury on itself.

Played Football With Immunity

Joey McN., after a quick indoctrination in the principles of Perfect Living, decided to apply the principles, insofar as he understood them, to a full year of football at a big college. He reported: "Perfect Living taught me to believe in my immunity to accident. I played in every minute of every game and never had time taken out once. Though we played teams that were plenty rough and tough, I never got a bruise or a scratch."

The broad concept of Perfect Living includes the tenet that the body knows all there is to know about its own chemical and physical functions, and also should know how to relate these functions to enduring the presence of a thinking conscious mind within the same person.

Enduring is the proper word here. Our bodies merely endure the co-presence of our minds. If, however, the conscious mechanism of the mind and the subconscious mechanisms of both mind and body succeed in getting together with mutual trust and interdependence, we then find ourselves on the threshold of Perfect Living.

Subduing a Creaky Floor

Did you ever observe yourself as you tried to walk quietly across a creaky floor? Your toes and the muscles of your feet seek to squeeze the very floor and try to muffle the creaky sounds. Your body balances itself delicately, trying to weigh less to reduce the noise further; and a hundred other unnamed muscles, ligaments, and tendons join in the action to try to aid the noiseless passage.

Your mind could never figure out how to subdue the creaky floor. Your mind, no matter how observant, could never recite all the body moves involved in the action. But all the while the Something Bigger inside you knows what it is doing, and the conscious mind wisely refrains from interfering.

Making Time Stand Still

Fear of yourself can turn into a tremendous asset in the immediate moment in which your very life is threatened; for example, when happily the two sides of you succeed in preventing a serious automobile accident. Here your will to live cooperates instantly with your mind. The mind sees the danger and recognizes it. The body, with all its unseen, unknown faculties, reacts in a perfect display of Self-Togetherness, with reflexes so sure and swift that for an instant time seems to stand still. You brake or turn the wheel or brace or do many other things you will marvel at once the danger is over.

You have demonstrated you can beat fear of yourself when you have to. And you wonder why you should ever harbor such fears of self as the following:

Sickness and Pain

Whether sickness and pain come from the outside or the inside, realize that there is a machine in your underground factory whose job it is to drive these ills away. Switch it on with the word "Change."

If the machine does not go to work at once, say "Change" often. Try saying: "Together—Change," or "Change—Together." Under no circumstances try to observe whether the distress is leaving at once. Just say "Change" and forget it. The sickness or trouble may have taken a long time to build up and needs proportionate time to fade away.

Forgetting, Misplacing

Examine your next act of forgetting a major item, or misplacing a needed article, and you will grant, on reflection, that some strange quirk of your own personality made you forget, caused you to misplace the article. Now if you have the ability for making yourself forget or misplace things, some other part of you should have the ability to prevent these errors. The switchword "Reach" is a big help in all these cases.

"Reach" and the machine for finding lost articles helped one woman to cure herself of the bad habit of forgetting and misplacing. When her finder machine finally got into perfect working order, she found she had been guided into the automatic habit of making a *second impression* on her conscious mind, each time she laid an object down. She was then equipped to use her old-fashioned memorizing memory for locating the misplaced objects quickly.

Fear of Body Functions

Though few of us spend much time in worrying how we bend a finger, there are other natural functions of the body that do receive too much attention, and interference, from the mind. An argument at mealtime can upset your digestion. Too much worry and excitement over your work can give you ulcers.

At one time or another in our lives, the rebel within assails us with "irregularity." Whether constipation is a result of fear of one's own body, or an act of resentment of one side of self against the other, or a combination of both, does not particularly matter. It is a real distress.

Sensational Success with SWIVEL

Dozens of investigators have found truly sensational results with a single switchword. In this instance the necessary requisites for personal automation are definitely present.

If you BELIEVE in your internal machinery and its responsiveness, all you need to do to produce the desired effect is say: SWIVEL.

"Something Bad Will Happen to Me."

Sometimes you make a mental photograph of yourself dying of cancer in a hospital, or suffering a heart attack behind the wheel of your car. The deadly part of such "premonitions" is the mental photograph. Your subconscious, misguided and running wild, may seize such a picture as an objective and in devious ways make the picture come true. *Important:* Erase every bad mental picture as soon as it appears. The switchword is: CANCEL.

Selfishness and Egomania

We often "reason" ourselves into selfishness and turn into raving maniacs trying to prove we are somebodys. With selfishness accepted as an objective, our powerful subconscious self cunningly offers to "cooperate" just to make trouble in the whole person. So we go "money-mad," "society-mad," "publicity-mad" or some other form of "mad." The switchword for the machine that corrects this awful state is: QUIET.

Tiredness

The switch for that tired feeling is: MOVE. The very same switch will help rid you of personal disorganization, such as inability to get out of the house in less than an hour before starting for work.

3. FEARS OF TIME

The subconscious soul, in its perverse role as the "enemy within," skillfully and perpetually tries to use time to harry our lives and destroy inner harmony.

Procrastination

To be always "putting things off," embracing inaction and waiting for things to straighten themselves out, produces unrest, self-blame, and misery.

The switchword for the procrastination-killing machine is: NOW. An attorney, widely admired by judges, clients, and the public is fondly known as "Now" McPherson.

Laziness

Laziness comes directly from the desire of everyone, every so often, to "kill time." But there is only one way to kill time, and *that is to use it*. If you can only get time on your side, and yourself on your own side, all fear of time will vanish from your heart. To dispel laziness via the automatic machinery inside your person, use the switch: GO.

Sinclair Lewis was a writer typical of the inward drive toward automation. Whenever and wherever his wife was renting new vacation headquarters for him, his only question would be: "Where do I work?"

Impatience

Impatience, literally intended to mean non-suffering, is one of our greatest sufferings. To realize how foolish it is to become impatient, try turning your watch ahead, or tear a few sheets off the calendar in your efforts to advance time. Why suffer the folly of impatience, when you have at your command an automatic machine designed to eradicate this form of self-torture? The switch is: SLOW.

Fear of the Deadline

The majority of people never bother about the deadline and that is why most jobs are delivered *after* they are promised. But others are so afraid they will never be able to get a job done in the time allotted, they refuse or contrive to avoid acceptance of the assignment and thus miss out on a world of accomplishment.

On the good side, there are a few members of society who always keep their time-promises to themselves and to others and go through life never missing a deadline. This is the small minority which views time as a close friend and regards the deadline as a real asset for finishing the job. Their switch is: DONE.

He Hesitated and Lost Until—

A report from a former deadline-fearer: "Deadlines always frightened me and I lost lots of business by failing to promise quick delivery. But when I began to switch on my underground machine for conquering the deadline, I noted a whole new approach to every job. Mentally I found myself going through the job in every detail before I even started it. When I now switch on my deadline machine with DONE, I can almost feel time standing still."

Getting Old Too Fast

Time is a measure of change, and change is inevitably thrown in our faces by the turn of the earth around itself to make a day and around the sun to make a year. After middle age, we are conscious of getting older with each successive heartbeat. Then our bodies, substantially under the control of our subterranean machinery, begin to suspect we are too old to live. To save your essential youth, no matter what the chronological facts are, switch on your youth-saving machine with the word: LEARN.

Many participants in Perfect Living experiments report that the switch "Learn" seemed to incline them to take up new studies. One began to learn French. Another started to practice the piano —an instrument he had forsaken in his youth. Interest in the new studies seemed to furnish all with a new lease on life.

4. FEARS OF FEAR

Fear, as a commodity to be feared, is even more elusive than time. We would like to put our hands on fear and choke it to death, but when we try to isolate fear we find it an "airy nothing." But though objective fear may have no discernible reality, subjective fear—the fear that boils inside you—is very real.

Tension, Hypertension, Nervousness

These are nicer words, fancier words, for fear of fear. It is much easier to say "I am nervous" than "I am terribly afraid, but of what I don't know." The machine that reduces tension in all forms is switched on with: COVER. Many individuals who heretofore would jump out of their boots if a firecracker exploded nearby or someone behind them suddenly said "Boo," report that by using the switch constantly, they now do not startle easily.

Worry

The tentacles of worry eventually reach out and grip all of us at some time or another.

When you are worried and confess your worries to your friends, they say: "Don't worry!" or "You shouldn't worry." Or they make jokes about the silly nature of worry.

You admit that something in particular is worrying you, but the biggest part of this worry is *fear of the unknown,* the negative surprises involved and the possibility of grave harm to you —none of which you can put your finger on right now.

The machine in your hidden equipment which can stop or greatly reduce worry is switched on with: BLUFF.

A college student in fear of flunking went into his exams, switching on his anti-worry machine, and passed with flying colors. A political employee, crowded into taking a lie detector test, boasts that he beat the lie detector with "Bluff."

Blue Mood

Some are inclined to have more blue streaks than others. They are always trying to depress themselves for no good reason. We all, on the occasion of a setback, have felt blue, and the blue streak sometimes endures long after we are able to remember the cause. But why try to explain any blue streak? Drive it away with: UP.

Loneliness

Loneliness is a singular example of fear of fear. You are afraid you are deserted. You may not be able to survive in a society that gives none of itself to you.

Now your loneliness-banishing machine, once switched on with: CIRCULATE, may not bring in a throng of friends tomorrow; but the machine will unveil the greatest of all friends, your other self. And that other self, once understood and appreciated, will automatically bring you the ineffable peace of heart which is Self-Togetherness.

The switch "Circulate" has been reported particularly effective when used in conjunction with "Together," as "Together—Circulate," or "Circulate—Together."

Frustration

Frustration is the direct result of Soul Number Two (the big you underneath) turning the tables on the Conscious You and nullifying its powers. In such a state neither of your two souls may succeed in downing the other. The inner contest is then an official "draw"—frustration. The machine to dissipate frustration is switched on with: OVER.

Fear of Failure, Consciousness of Cowardice

For one provable success we are inwardly conscious of a hundred failures. If there were no available means for reducing this fear and it kept on piling up, it would finally smother the will to live in all of us. Most experimenters, who have used the switch Bluff to overcome their fear of failure find themselves confessing (and boasting) publicly: "I am a coward and I admit it, but I want to be a winning coward and not a loser."

17

THE
MIRACLE
OF THE SUPER-SELF

We HAVE SEEN AND HEARD OF MANY MIRACLES HAPPEN-
ing when belief, true and complete belief, was present. Belief alone in many cases has been enough to deliver the good
that was wanted and needed. In all walks of life, the man who
believes and never falters in his self-confidence comes out on top.

And what is confidence? Literally it means "belief with." With
what? It has to mean belief with yourself, belief in yourself. Now
reason alone can never produce confidence all by itself. We can
prove to ourselves that we ought to win, that winning is better
than losing, and then, after playing the game, we lose anyhow.
The conscious mind may outline the framework of belief but it
cannot make you believe.

The subsurface self, which is really the great super-self, must
produce and sustain the belief. Surely we will all concede that
when belief is present the emotions are at work, many of them so

subtle and complicated we cannot announce which emotion is doing most in behalf of belief.

Always Present in Perfect Living

If we can find out how to create belief in that part of ourselves which is the all-powerful part, then we have the kind of belief that is necessary to deliver Perfect Living.

Belief must be present in every project, small or large. You must know you *actually know how* to relieve yourself of any distress or accomplish any desire. And you *do* know *once you believe you know*. Refer again to the misplaced or lost article you are searching for. You KNOW you know where it is, and though you cannot announce with your lips or put into words its location, you still know you know the answer. And you believe you know. So a study of the anatomy of belief should quickly strengthen your believing abilities.

In all matters of belief, the conscious mind properly applied and in healthy condition, has all the believing vigor it needs in life. It is the great you underneath that is in dire need of belief-development.

Thus your subsurface soul loves formulas instead of facts. It loves to do tricks because it believes in the how-to principle behind the trick. It loves form whether it sees it in a baseball player or a public speaker. It loves the multiplication tables, recognizing the various formulas of mathematics as simple principles for arriving at thousands of new answers. A sure-fire formula is power.

The Sub-You Is a Ritualist

The sub-you believes in power. Like a dog who becomes a minor ritualist in his daily habits, your subconscious, and all the other facets of the under-the-surface you, is inclined to ritualism on the things it believes in.

Get this side of your self more and more subject to formula, whether in the metaphysical, the physical, or the psychological realm. The engineer believes in his slide rule and that one device makes him subconsciously a great believer.

He Takes His Slide Rule to Social Shindigs

One engineer confides: "I take my slide rule (it is small and compact) with me wherever I go, especially to social affairs where on first thought it could never be useful. But it is a talisman, a good luck piece, which gives me extraordinary confidence.

"I stick my hand in my pocket and touch it when the conversation gets on subjects that are over my head, and this absolute belief in my slide rule, gives me confidence to cope with any subject, strange, new, or baffling. Believing in it absolutely, I have come to believe in myself at all times."

"I Can Do Anything!"

Difficult goals are more easily believed in by the subsurface you. When you take an "impossible" objective like "I'll make a million dollars in the next five years," your conscious side refuses to believe. Your subsurface side takes a wide-open stand on the matter. Finding the conscious can prove the goal is "impossible," it begins to sulk, or rebel, and thus you are split apart. One part of you is sorry it ever brought the matter up.

A good antidote for non-belief in general is the reputation of the statement: "I can do anything! I can do anything!" Such a statement is, of course, more acceptable to your subconscious self than to your conscious self which, if allowed to contemplate the impossibilities, will reason you out of any such belief.

Example: When you say "Every day in every way, I am getting better and better!" your conscious mind answers by asking, "Where? How? Show me some proof!" But if the statement is repeated over and over a thousand times, the advocates of auto-suggestion maintain that eventually the truth will soak in, belief will grow strong, and the *belief* will actually *make you better*. There is certainly enough evidence to indicate that auto-suggestion has been remarkably effective in many persons and many cases. And reflection on the very meaning of "auto" (self) will point out that there are two sides of you involved in the process, the big side, your underside, and the little side, your conscious mind.

Belief Is Not a Conscious Act

Belief has been wrongly emphasized as a conscious act. True belief is essentially subconscious, subsurface, and not the product of reason. The religion you follow so faithfully was successfully drilled into you in your earliest years, even before you reached "the age of reason." By bypassing the conscious mind, your faith was developed almost completely in your subconscious, which clings to it with unshakable ardor and will not let your conscious mind dwell very long on any doubts or disbeliefs.

Thus subconscious belief is a thousand times as strong as conscious belief. Practice at throwing the full weight of your belief over to your subconscious side especially on matters which your conscious mind denounces and can refute. When your conscious says: "There can't be flying saucers because time, distance, speed, and limits of matter cannot substantiate any such theory," answer by telling yourself: "Anything is possible which is not self-contradictory." Or say: "How could everyone of thousands of people who say they saw them be mistaken?" Put up an argument (in faith) with this reasonable, logical side of yourself: "Just for the fun of it, let's say both sides of me believe in flying saucers. What can we lose!" Try any number of experiments, and use variety in so doing, to steal the believing role away from your conscious mind, and put it into the domain of your super-self.

Some Easy Ways to Begin Believing

1. *In All Matters of Belief, Submit to Your Bigger Self.* Apply yourself especially to enjoying acceptance of the things which the conscious mind finds it hard to believe in. To get in the believing mood, try being "gullible." Believe the ads, say "yes" to every claim. Believe the teller of tall tales, especially when it costs you nothing and you lose no money. Contradiction, skepticism, criticism and debate are practices in *disbelief*. These faults, practiced so constantly and relentlessly, stunt our believing ability.

2. *Initiative Induces Belief; Persistence Increases It.* You may consciously announce: "I could never write a book!" Think of the millions of people who have said, "I have so much material, I could write a book," and yet never did. They did not actually believe they could.

If you flippantly think you could write a book, go ahead and start it, though your belief in your ability to complete the job is nil. *Begin* it, and from deep down inside you comes the first spark of belief. *Continue* and belief grows minute by minute. Invoke undying persistence and your book will see the light of day. And full credit to the completed job must be given to the belief in yourself and in your ability to do what at first seemed impossible.

3. *Refrain From Criticizing and Believe for at Least Half an Hour.* If you want to see how easy it is to engender a believing mood, on occasion deliberately refrain from finding fault with people and with things in general.

The more intelligent you are, the harder this is to do but conversely, the more beneficial to inner harmony.

Anyone who is halfway smart is a critic and a fault-finder. It pays, once in awhile, to deliberately forfeit your critical ability, your powers of observation, your intellectual prowess, and not only *act* dumb but *be* dumb.

If you are hypercritical in what you read, try reading and accepting every line as the gospel truth. When a dumb move or foolish mistake of a fellow worker causes you anger or distress, try telling yourself: "He is the smart one, I am the dumb one."

Believe wholeheartedly every pseudo-fact or item of misinformation that is aimed at you. You can believe it all for at least half an hour.

Do not, of course, follow this experiment all your life, but the process, indulged in for half an hour at a time, invariably strengthens your believing faculty. Also, as seen in our chapter on submission, the unwarranted believing, in knowingly invoking a forfeit of intelligence, tends to humiliate the surface you and thus produces temporary togetherness with the sub-you. When the sub-you, on occasion, is brought to believe what the surface you knows is wrong, it will be more willing in normal living to believe what the surface you knows is right.

His Professor Made Him Sick

One student of very high I.Q. writes: "I have a professor who annoys me to the point of actually making me sick. He does not know the subject he is teaching and is constantly making statements and giving opinions that are completely inaccurate and often downright false.

"On impulse I resolved, each time I went into his class, to believe everything he said. It was only one hour a week and I figured I could not hurt myself too much with the experiment.

"That hour a week has now turned into sheer paradise—not because I am now believing so many things that are not true but because the positive act of believing had downed my negative tendency for fault-finding.

"Now I get along fine with the prof and much better with my fellow students. My belief potential has been increased immensely and in training myself to believe non-essential errors I have often discovered that there is real truth buried somewhere in these same 'errors'."

4. *Formulas Versus Evidence.* The BIG You, underneath, is never too enthusiastic about facts or evidence. The conscious mind always respects evidence whether it pertains to facts assimilated in the past or facts which face you in the present. As you dwell on a major factor that may disturb or change your living, you invariably feel some disturbing non-belief inside you that seems to deny the fact.

Some people, at the time of a sudden and unexpected death in the family, actually disbelieve that the beloved is dead. It takes time for the awful fact to seep into the subconscious and deep down into the subterranean passages of experience. For this is a *first* experience, and the subconscious is serious in groping with all first experiences. On the other hand, your conscious mind accepts the incontrovertible fact of death, of accident, of loss, and all other clean-cut facts because it is primarily designed to operate on facts and the truth derived from facts.

5. *Adopt a "Second Religion."* One's second religion is sometimes referred to as "hobby," "avocation," "favorite game," "forte," "crusade," "ideal" or a wide variety of other titles.

One's religion, in the meaning of religious worship, can seldom be enough unless that religion be embraced totally by bringing the worshipper into the formal religious life. Priests, ministers, nuns and religious brothers often find a second religion absolutely necessary. We are led to think that these noble people who sacrifice everything for God have found the way to contentment. But they are all human beings regardless of the vows they have taken. They are subject, like all humans, to lonesomeness, to temper, to mean thoughts, to weaknesses of the flesh.

We have seen many of these religious people embrace art and become extremely competent in this most difficult of all fields. If pure religion were enough, if the glory of God were enough for their individual and dedicated lives, they would have no need for art, or for collecting rare objects, or making things with their hands. Their tendency to take on a second religion is evidence of an unconscious need to strengthen their belief in God and in the strict, hard life to which they are dedicated.

They Kidded Him About His Second Religion

A devout and religious man, publicly and privately living his religion to the absolute letter, was often kidded by his children for giving so much more time to his second religion than to his first. His second religion was the union labor movement in which he was a pioneer. Every ounce of his physical and mental energy seemed to go into unionism. He held every job in his union at various times but never once drew a dollar in salary. Later he became the second man in the labor union movement in North America to be named a president emeritus.

As he grew old, his children would joke about his failing memory on family matters but to the end his memory on labor history was phenomenal. In the year of his final sickness he wrote a comprehensive book covering a fifty-year span of labor events entirely from memory.

Hubby's Hobby Too Expensive

A worthy hobby keeps many a person contented with life. But the hobbyist's wife, noting the expense of the hobby, is tempted to interfere. In most cases she cannot because her husband's belief and immersion in his hobby withstand all assaults of reason or expediency.

Few men can retire and live long without a second religion. Some of us, while young and strong, say: "My work is my hobby." But work alone is dangerous as an all-consuming hobby. Old age takes it away from you. Changes in economic events can cause you to lose interest. But when you have given great amounts of time and money to a hobby cultivated over the years, it is impossible to lose interest. The hobby keeps you studying, growing, and makes the future worthwhile. When one has too few things left to believe in, fear of death, the end of living, moves in with its terror and agony.

6. *Cherish the Memory of Your Childhood Achievements.* Though you perhaps consider yourself a person of mediocre achievement, an honest examination will disclose many events in your personal history which produced and confirmed belief. Accomplishments of your early years, especially, provide clean-cut examples of the power of belief. "I made a tablecloth when I was nine years old and it was a fine thing." "I recited the Declaration of Independence word for word when I was in fourth grade of grammar school."

You did some odd but noteworthy thing as a child and drew the acclaim of the adult world around you. Though others have forgotten, these feats are still within the grasp of your own memory. Recall them. Dwell on them. Resurrect the exact feeling you had when long ago you were praised for these accomplishments.

You can feel power, belief, invincibility resurging within you. For when you were great, in however small a matter, you achieved that greatness by believing in the extraordinary powers you had then, *powers which you still possess.*

7. *Believe in Your Instincts.* These powers surprised you as a child because they were "buried" powers. You did not identify them as automatic machinery. But you can, if you wish, now recognize them as essential equipment in your personal underground factory.

The Shot Completed Before Begun

Ben Hogan, when in his heyday as Number One golfer of the world, insisted that as he addressed a golf ball to make a shot, he could so·concentrate that *he saw the shot completed* even before he moved his club head toward the ball.

Who can possibly announce the thousand and one items involved in a single act of skill? Babe Ruth, in his entire baseball career, never once threw the ball to the wrong base. He followed instinct. And Ruth's instincts worked because he believed in them.

8. *Believe in Emotional Proof.* If you believe in your doctor, he is a good doctor for you; if you do not believe, his medicine or advice will never work. Doctor-belief is generated by your watching his hands, liking the sound of his voice, the sense of his words; observing the impressive equipment in his office. All this is emotional proof—far from logic and reason. The very chemistry of his presence works on your own chemistry to elicit your belief. And most of your cure comes from belief in the man. Otherwise, why should a *placebo,* a dummy pill with no chemicals in it, work so often?

9. *Believe in the Best.* In all second religions the best is the driving force. The sports follower wants to look at the pro. The individual competitor seeks nothing less than victory. The idealist idolizes the best of all possible ages; he insists records were made to be broken.

Self-Togetherness is the VERY BEST first goal you can set for yourself. To accept it as your first goal is pure belief. With enough reflection the two sides of you find it easy to accept, as the BEST THING IN LIFE.

Experimenters Report on Perfect Living Beliefs

Some comments from believers who have felt the magic of Perfect Living:

"Let me try to tell you what it feels like to be together with one's self. It is like receiving good news every minute of every hour; good news, nothing but constant good news."

"I liken it to young love, which doesn't last forever but is pure heaven while it does."

From a Breadwinner

"Like everyone else I have had my share of fine moments, only to have the grand feeling vanish on any kind of a reverse. The prolonged happy period, however, can best be described as a state of *invulnerability.*

"I seem to put on a coat of armor, weightless and elevating, which shields me from every kind of bad feeling, every kind of fear. I then like to tell myself that this feeling is a natural state to which I am entitled because my true belief gives me such right to feel so carefree. This is no world of make-believe because I am still the family breadwinner, I have to drive my car as carefully as ever, I have to pay out real money to buy groceries."

Afraid of Becoming a Dumbbell?

Another report: "I had a deal of trouble believing in the principles enunciated under Submission. Wasn't there danger in telling myself I was dumb, that I did not deserve any credit for my formal education, my hard-won reputation? As I went to bed one night after a bitter row with a traffic policeman, I knew I couldn't sleep. Rehashing the incident and the injustice I had received, I started in with endless planning for revenge.

"I could actually feel my blood pressure going up, hear my heart pumping so loudly it startled me. In the depths of this senseless excitement, I saw I was actually punishing *myself.* I conceded that because my conscious mind felt so right and sure of itself, my subconscious was running riot with my whole mind and body, in protest perhaps, or perhaps just for the hell of it."

He asked himself for mercy. "It then became clear that the policeman was not the cause of my excitement, but that I myself was the cause, through sheer ignorance and stupidity.

"I then began begging my second self to take pity, to render mercy, as if I were appealing to a higher authority. It was at this point that I found the word-switch that turns on the machine for quelling such unjustified excitement. I started saying, 'Uncle,' 'Uncle.' I immediately fell into a peaceful sleep and next morning could scarcely remember any of the details of the traffic fuss."

Belief Nourishes Further Belief

As you proceed more earnestly into Perfect Living, individual switches and individual machines will let you down on occasion. But though you are an outright skeptic, you will test a few switches, perhaps just to prove the system will not work. Of course, pure belief, sharp want, clear objective, and a state of Self-Togetherness are essentials before the switches can be asked to do their job, but they often work anyhow, just to intrigue skeptics.

Fallen Arch Mended, Fear of High Places Quelled

A believer was chatting with a man from Toronto, Canada, and a man from Lebanon in the lobby of a great New York Hotel. They were attending a World Congress for the Crippled and Physically Handicapped. Though neither of these gentlemen was handicapped physically, one confessed that he had been walking with a limp for several months "because the arch on one foot had fallen."

The other, in the candid warmth of Perfect Living atmosphere, admitted that he was intensely afraid of high places and could not climb a flight of stairs without developing as bad a case of nerves.

A skimpy explanation of the theory of the switches followed. It was suggested that the sore-foot man say "Change" and the high-place-fearer say "Adjust" for the high place and "Ho" to relieve any nervous tension with a sigh.

Next day in great excitement came the victims, reporting. The sore-foot man had said "Change," felt the sole of his sore foot, found there a small hard callus which was making him limp. He removed it and the pain was all gone! The high-place-fearer said: "I faced a high flight of stairs, said 'Adjust' and ran up. I now felt no fear only a little tense. But then I said 'Ho,' sighed, and was not in the least bit nervous."

Make ten tests of the Perfect Living Principles. Two of these ten tests have a good chance of working though you are not yet properly indoctrinated. Success will come in a given number of tries, and it will not come under the aegis of religion, mesmerism, occultism, or preternaturalism of any kind. It will come *naturally,* so that whatever your religion or non-religion, your belief will be nourished and amplified by proof *that happens to you.*

18

HOW

TO SATISFY

YOUR EVERY DESIRE

Emerson SAID: "BE VERY CAREFUL WHAT YOU SET YOUR HEART UPON, FOR YOU WILL SURELY HAVE IT."

He was emphasizing how important it is to choose the right objective, for if your great subconscious wants the wrong thing, it will get the wrong thing for the whole person.

"Be Very Careful
What You Set Your Heart Upon"

He Wanted $500,000

Take the case of F.C., who went money-mad. He decided he wanted to make $500,000 in a few years. The term "money-mad" fitted him perfectly; he began to want money so bad it became a form of insanity. He began to save money, down to pennies, with a zeal that was almost vicious. He skipped meals, newspapers, buses, all amusements.

Within a year, so avid was his saving and so astonishing his want, that long extra hours of labor and small-scale investment brought him the money to start an automobile agency. With tremendous passion and amazing speed he built the agency into a flourishing business and in two years of prodigious, applied *want* walked right into his first nervous breakdown.

He Broke Down as He Reached His Goal

It took a few months to recover from this breakdown, but he did. And right away he resumed his passionate money-making activities, only to fall into another physical breakdown (from overwork) two years later—just as he had reached his goal of $500,000!

He had made it. He had it. But his health was wrecked, and his objective, though accomplished, had brought him to the sickbed he never left for the next six years till he died.

She Prayed to Assume Her Brother's Pain

A woman whose brother had suffered a terrible automobile accident actually prayed to God to relieve her dear brother of his terrible pain and give it to her instead. She died shortly thereafter of a combination of major heart ailments.

Where Did All the People Go?

A doctor spent his best early years in trying to see how much money he could make. Patients were hustled in and out of his office as if on a conveyor line. He never had time to talk to them about their personalities or problems; in fact, though he served many for several years, he could not even tell their names if he met them on the street. This doctor made his million, and made it fast, and now in middle age and "taking it easy" is wondering why he cannot enjoy people, hasn't any friends, and is unable to talk in human terms about a single subject under the sun.

Be very careful what you set your heart upon, especially if you follow the system of want which is based on concentrated passion. Passionate want does get fast results, and very often reaches the wrong goal.

If the objective involves tremendous stress, self-conquest, relentless application, the agent of this extraordinary want can fall a victim to want in the stark nature of *madness*.

But Want Is Still Necessary

We can all do very well without want-madness, yet some degree of want is necessary in every program of personal improvement, in every project aimed at delivering some good to the seeker.

But, we may state as a certainty that more people lose out on life's thrills and recompenses by not having wants than by having them.

Eight "Black Beasts"

Various factors knock down the possibility of wants entering your system. A few black beasts that discourage want are:

1. Work

Of a new kind, challenging to your weakness and inexperience, work too enormous in volume, work for which you have not the time (you say). *Sample:* "I ought to write a book," or "I could write a play." If you ever bring yourself to want to write the work, you will.

2. Meeting People

Old contacts, friends whom you ought to call on for help in your projects; friends who have political power which can get you favors; your dislike of bringing old friends and acquaintances into your projects. And new people—your hatred of approaching them with self-advantage in mind, fear of rebuffs, laughter, ridicule, insults, their non-compliance.

The more sensitive and self-conscious the person, the more intelligent he is, as a rule. But fear of mixing with others in matters of business or other forms of production, robs the public at large of the benefits of the gifted party.

Very often, for one stranger who would rebuff a newcomer with an attractive proposition, four others would be interested in entertaining it. Nearly everyone would like to be a salesman, and though not formally occupied in definite sales work, would like to be identified as having outstanding sales gifts. But fear of confronting people stifles the *want* to sell!

3. Fear of Loss

The want may turn out to be a drawback instead of an asset. If, for instance, you hate to make speeches, or write letters, and the contemplated objective involves these projects, you are inclined to bypass the want that gets you into unpleasant activity.

4. Inertia

Inertia is more pleasant than want because it apparently involves no effort. But you lose inertia in a fire, a fight, physical danger, because the want to get out of the danger or harm is really an escape towards, or a preservation of, the old inertia—the *status quo.*

5. Resting on Laurels

You tell yourself you have done pretty well in the past and past performances should be enough to satisfy you. Useless recounting of past achievements tends to slow down further want.

6. Resentment at Personal Reform

Examples: dieting, or giving up alcohol or tobacco. Your subconscious rebels at the thought. Sometimes, however, in your contemplation of the "enormity" of the sacrifice, your subconscious decides to give up something else, such as candy, as a sop to your duty toward reform of some kind. Thus in the forfeiture of wanting bigger things, you end up with a definite smaller want.

7. Hoping, Wishing

You try to tell yourself you can get a worthy objective by hoping, wishing, praying, waiting for luck—everything but want! The greatest prayer of all is a want in itself, and the luckiest individual of all is he who has acquired a definite want.

8. Letting Others Arrange Your Wants

Such a plan depends on others being interested in your material success, your practical happiness. But few really care about you; everybody is too much wrapped up in himself. However, people often are indirectly responsible for your wants.

It is almost universally true that a man makes more money and earns a higher salary after he marries. Marriage proves to him that he needs more money than formerly, and get it he does—just because he wants it.

Sometimes the want of another becomes unbearable to the observer and thus the observer becomes a walking depository of the same want.

Builder Fred wanted his brother Joe to put up the money for a new building. Joe did not like the idea and refused flatly. But Fred went to a third party, a mutual friend of the builder and his brother, and poured forth a vibrant description of the contemplated building and the reason for its existence.

The third party, Vince, imbued with Fred's overpowering want, went to Joe and with added want of his own induced him to put up the money.

Ultimately the project missed fire and everyone lost money, but real want had its way anyhow.

Six Elements of True Want

1. *"Newness," Immediacy.* A want postponed for some future occasion is no want at all.

2. *The Deliberate Elimination of All Arguments Against the Want.* A person must be arbitrary, ruthless, in embracing a want and not consider the reasons why the want should be passed up.

3. *Embracing of the Want for the Want's Sake Instead of for Comfort's Sake.* There must be the feeling of work, of turmoil, of possible defeat, of suffering involved in every want. Love the want and want it over and above all discomfort and negative feeling.

4. *Give Yourself to the Want.* Put the best part of yourself into the want, "shoot the works." Every true want must be a 100 percent want.

5. *Rationality, and Perfect Planning Must Not be Over-stressed.* Reason of itself cannot make wants; in fact every true want is essentially unreasonable. Follow your instincts, your sub-surface nature, rather than your intellect. You cannot stop to figure out whether or not the want is foolish. If the objective is solid enough, if its attainment is difficult enough, all you need is the want to get you there.

6. *All Wants Seem to Have an Element of Strangeness, For-eignness.* You seem to have never been there before, never wanted anything like this before. The ways and means you will use are all unknown at present and strange things will happen in the process of realizing your goal. But the very strangeness of the operation is one of its greatest appeals. Every want is a new adventure.

How Want Can Attack Another Want

Pain is a definite sign of Apartness of the individual. Pain is notification to the person that he is living imperfectly. In our abhorrence of pain, we often attest our startling demand for perfection in our sensitive systems. Thus we essentially attest the fact that we bring this pain on ourselves, and actually *WANT THE PAIN* far more than we want its cessation.

A pain that stays too long may have been wanted all the while; but suddenly you notice that it disappears after a tenancy of several months. You "forgot" about it, you say, and thus got rid of it. But actually you got rid of it because, being disgusted with it, you began to want its disappearance far more than you wanted its continuance.

Healthy People Hate Hospitals

The hypochondriac wants to stay sick because it pleases him to be able to tell of doctors' visits, of pains and aches. The healthy man dreads the thought of wasting long hours in doctors' waiting rooms, the humiliation of taking medicine and pills, and being in a hospital. He wants to stay well, imagining how disgusting it is to be sick.

This proves that *if an objective is completely accepted by the person as a real and a worthy objective the irresistible force of true want automatically arises and goes to work*—without any help from the mind of the individual, and without any formal and conscious report by his senses.

Draw a Picture—a Good Picture

Mentally draw the correct picture. If you are a policeman and decide you want to be chief, make a mental photograph of yourself in the chief's uniform. If you are a schoolteacher and you want to be superintendent, project yourself mentally into the superintendent's office, sitting at the superintendent's desk. If you want to be a nurse, mentally don a nurse's uniform. If you want to own an airplane, or be a millionaire, or have a castle in some foreign country—just draw a mental picture and religiously hold that picture foremost in your heart—in the same way you took a picture of your sweetheart to your heart in your courtship days. Such a picture held closely enough, kept forever in both your conscious mind and your subconscious, will surely guide you and all your abilities into the correct channels for reaching your objective.

Be sure the picture is the best picture for your own best interest. Beware of wrong pictures or pictures that portray accidents or evil intentions. Once the picture is created in your mind, you will find yourself stating both silently to yourself, and outwardly to whoever will listen, your firm objective for reaching your goal.

Time may be required. The more difficult the objective, the more time will be necessary. This is why you must forever hold the picture foremost in your inner vision, never relinquishing its prominence or its clearness in your own mind. Often it will be necessary to prompt your own imagination to recreate the picture and bring up its vision in new clearness and sharpness.

Preliminary Moves

Practice getting acquainted with your "wanting" powers. Experiment with a few relatively unimportant wants. Want a new pair of shoelaces or a new set of rubber heels. These items may have been neglected by you; now tell yourself you want them. Better still, draw a mental picture of these fresh wants and try giving them a constant and foremost position in your mind. There's no doubt about it, the objective will be quickly reached.

Now try a few "not want to's," such as the elimination of bad habits. Instead of smoking you may decide to picture yourself chewing gum when ordinarily you would be smoking. You will find your automatic machinery will be glad to take over rather quickly if you trust to it completely and give it a definite assignment.

The magical powers of this machinery are demonstrated very clearly on the "morning after" you have indulged too freely on the night before.

Strange Foods on the "Morning After"

In the throes of a hangover, the body knows it needs food and nourishment, and strangely is also clearly aware that it does not desire the "usual thing." When your stomach is upset, you may find yourself seeking the oddest kind of food, things you may not have touched for months. Say "Together" and let yourself go where you will. You may find yourself eating cole slaw or pop corn or drinking large quantities of pure water, all because the *real you* knows far better what your body now needs than does the rational you.

Make a Manifesto

If both your inner and outer selves decide that something is good for you, an objective without contest from your ordinarily warring selves, the objective should be acted on at once, because it carries all the miraculous powers of Self-Togetherness. In this mood *make a manifesto*.

A manifesto is a public announcement of either a sensational or serious nature, telling the world you are going to do something, something indeed difficult, well-nigh "impossible." The world will not necessarily pay too much attention to your "impossible" declaration, but you will hear your own voice uttering the pronouncement, and the sound of your own voice will give you added confidence and resolution. Do not merely utter your manifesto out loud; put it in the form of writing and send it to all interested parties. Be sure your audience will remember what you have declared you will do, so if you are tempted to quit, one or two witnesses confirm the impossibility of your objective and thus agitate you to new fervor and resolution.

Couldn't Sing, Whistle or Play a Note, but Wrote a Song Hit

Invite the scoffer and the skeptic to challenge you. One young man who could not sing or play a note of music was laughingly told he could never write a popular song. But he proceeded to make up the tune in his head, composed the words and struggled with a professional arranger a whole day in trying to sing his song in such a way that the arranger could write down the true notes. In two weeks the song came out and became a universal hit.

In a game when you face an impossible shot, all that is often necessary is for your opponent to chortle at your discomfiture and assume the shot is impossible. You often make it—to prove him a liar.

19

A KEY
FOR EVERY LOCK

Our DIRECT INVESTIGATIONS AND EXPERIMENTS IN
Perfect Living have extended over a period of at least ten
years. The author's other independent studies in the many
intriguing fields of parapsychology have extended over at least
forty-five years and have involved contacts and work with thousands of individuals in many different classes and occupations.

In the specific studies of Perfect Living and attendant tests
and experiments, we have dealt with high school students, college
students, school and college teachers, principals, social center directors, personnel directors, servicemen, businessmen, office and
factory employees, sales directors, salesmen, patients in bed, sick
people, happy people, sad people, frustrated people, positive and
negative thinkers, men, women, young men and young women—
just about anyone who had an open mind and was willing to try
something new.

There is a universal desire in all types, ages, and dispositions
of people to find a better way to live. There is a wholesome and

ready acceptance of the possibility of Perfect Living. One is never at want for helpers, testers, experimenters, researchers—and believers!

A List of Switchwords

Since it would be impossible to publish a book big enough to contain all the details of each and every successful case history, we will list here the several word switches which have worked near miracles in hundreds upon hundreds of cases. This is your open invitation to sample the system. Just try a few of the switches in your different attempts to realize a personal desire or eliminate a distress. After a very few tests, you will find a switch which works and thus draws you into a more intensive study and acceptance of the system. No attempt has been made to classify the switches by the jobs they do, either alphabetically or generically. The job is stated first, the switch at the end of each statement.

To create new ideas—*ON*.

To reduce smoking—*COUNT*.

To get in mood for writing—*GIGGLE*.

To stay young and to look young immediately—*LEARN*.

To be a good mechanic—*CONSIDER*.

To break a bad habit—*OFF*.

To meet a deadline—*DONE*.

To sigh—*HO*.

To win in a competitive game—*FIGHT*.

To upset an opponent in such a game—*FIGHT*.

To achieve moderation in any field where tempted to excess—*CUT*.

To display pep and sudden energy—*MOVE*.

To turn a setback into an uplift—*ELATE*.

To remember, in sense of memorize—*CARE*.

To remember something forgotten—*REACH*.

To find lost or misplaced article—*REACH*.

To solve a problem—*REACH*.

To prevent a person or action from annoying one—*CANCEL*.

To obliterate a negative thought—*CANCEL*.

To dispel a worry—*CANCEL*.

To sell—*GIVE*.

To acquire skill—*WATCH*.

To love to read—*JUDGE*.

To maintain good health—*BE*.

To be kind—*TINY*.

To invent—*REACH*.

To relieve constipation—*SWIVEL*.

To heal a scab—*ALONE*.

To stop drinking—*SAVE*.

To keep a resolution—*DONE*.

To destroy remorse—*TOMORROW*.

To cease regretting—*THANKS*.

To secure transportation—*ON*.

To smile—*NAME OF A KNOWN SMILER*.

To stand up straight—*NAME OF A KNOWN STRAIGHT-UP STANDER*.

To enthuse—*NAME OF A FAMILIAR ENTHUSIAST.*

To cure hypersensitivity—*DUCK.*

To prevent pouting streak—*POSTPONE.*

To handle anything unpleasant—*ADJUST.*

To dispel an attack of the blues—*UP.*

To act on good impulse—*NOW.*

To stop faultfinding—*PRAISE.*

To build will power—*DONE.*

To banish lonesomeness—*BE.*

To get rid of inertia—*MOVE.*

To avoid poverty or debt—*CANCEL.*

To nourish ambition—*ON.*

To eliminate procrastination—*DO.*

To promote—*FOR.*

To advertise—*SCHEME.*

To secure publicity—*RIDICULOUS.*

To retain good feeling or sense of well-being—*STRETCH*

To assume or carry a burden—*ADJUST.*

To get something out of eye—*CHANGE.*

To dispel ache or pain in any part of body—*CHANGE.*

To turn on personality—*CHUCKLE.*

To turn on politeness or courtesy—*TINY.*

To convert another—*TAP.*

To dispel nervousness—*BLUFF.*

To dispel conscious fear—*BLUFF*.

To call forth extra personal ability—*DIVINE*.

To preserve personal safety—*GUARD*.

To make yourself beautiful or handsome—*PRAISE*.

To acquire good taste—*COPY*.

To keep a secret—*FOREVER*.

To subdue inner excitement—*COVER*.

To get to sleep—*OFF*.

To build—*PUT*.

To dress better—*SPEND*.

To find percentage—*ADD*.

To learn a secret—*WAIT*.

To improve your mental telepathy—*BETWEEN*.

To swim—*CONTINUE*.

To withstand impatience—*SLOW*.

To handle success—*SUFFER*.

To handle prosperity—*SUFFER*.

To avoid carelessness—*ATTENTION*.

To improve perspective—*AROUND*.

To build character—*HOLD*.

To ward off apartness of the personality just as negative factor is entering—*UNCLE*.

To develop or increase endurance—*CONTINUE*.

To be wise—*SLOW*.

To achieve peace of conscience—*BE*.

To build, produce—*ON*.

To develop leadership—*TAKE*.

To build a fortune—*FIND*.

To make money—*COUNT*.

To develop courage—*SWING*.

To read the future—*LISTEN*.

To work miracles—*DIVINE*.

To do anything—*TOGETHER*.

To lose inferiority complex—*UP*.

To become an orator—*ACT*.

To publish a successful newspaper—*PERSONAL*.

To publish a successful magazine—*SOPHISTICATE*.

To make your children obedient—*CROWD*

To be compatible with others—*WITH*.

To be soothing to others—*SWEET*.

To be pious—*SHOW*.

To complete a lot of detailed work—*NEXT*.

To create appeal—*HOLE*.

To design—*SCHEME*.

To appear rich—*WASTE*.

To create beauty—*CURVE*.

To appear cultured—*CLASSIC*.

To help others—*GIVE*.

To bury your grudges—*REVERSE*.

To reduce your bragging—*DOWN*.

To lose pettiness—*MAGNANIMITY*.

The Switch—"Together"

Many casual experimenters who have only scratched the surface in their study of Perfect Living have reported their trouble in remembering the specific switches for particular distresses and desires. They have found themselves resorting to the simple word "Together" as the one and only switch for attaining any and all objectives.

Many of these investigators have had phenomenal success with the word "Together" as a means of switching on all their various hidden machines of experience; they swear by its magic. And it is true that the beginner, with just a smattering of knowledge of the new system, gets so many encouraging results from the use of the switchword "Together," he does not go any further with his experiments or studies. The professional exponent of Perfect Living, after having achieved sufficient acquaintance with the automatic system and having undergone a wealth of tests and studies, eventually will develop the automatic faculties that will make "Together" the master switch for his whole underground experience factory. No other switchword will be necessary.

Much Practice Required

But before this state is reached, a great deal of practice must be turned in. For though "Together" may deliver amazing results for newcomers, it tends to lose its efficacy—at least in early stages—for doing a large variety of specific jobs in distress-banishment or desire-accomplishment.

But never lose your faith in the magic word "Together." Know it for certain as the master switch for your underground experience factory which has all the automatic equipment for Perfect Living.

Give to this system the same devotion, application, time and hard work you have given to any other of the age-old systems that have been offered to you as a solution for correct living. Give it as much as you give to a hobby. Then the word "Together" will ultimately be the only switch you will ever need for living a life free of fret and failure.

20

THE
MIND-MACHINES
IN ACTION

Let US NOT CLASSIFY THIS NEW SYSTEM IN ANY WAY with unproven (in the sense of undemonstrable) phenomena like extrasensory perception or mental telepathy. Telepathy happens often, to be sure, but never under artificial control. In fact, psychokinesis (the combining of mind with matter to break physical laws) is much more common than mental telepathy. In the case of gifted individuals (not necessarily "psychic," but certainly ones with "something on the ball"), psychokinesis comes closer to falling under control in the right hands.

The theory of Perfect Living, properly practiced, can deliver a definite measure of control by the individual over his present and his future. What the world might call "miracles" if they had been wrought by mystery, supernatural invocation, or other phenomenal means, become ordinary happenings under the aegis of Perfect Living.

Four Basic Conditions

In every case of a Perfect Living performance, one must always remember the four basic conditions that are required of the worker:

1. *Submission to Self-Union*
2. *Objective and Want*
3. *Belief*
4. *The Switch*

In the beginning of your many experiments, you will tend to forget these simple requirements. Often you will be so astonished at the immediate results of what seems like an aimless test, you will elate over your discoveries and want to dispense with the requirements. But do not be tempted to throw away your tools, especially in the first stages of your scientific progress. Repeat the necessities over and over: Submission to the bigger You; want, really *want* your objective and state it so clearly that you can have no doubt about it. *Believe;* select the proper switch and flip it as you would an electric light switch, spending no time or thought on its meaning.

CASE:
A Thousand "Toothaches" in the Back

Subject was an artist about fifty-five years old. He had never been troubled with arthritis or arthritic tendencies. But after a siege of critical sickness—the flu and pneumonia—he passed through a period of joyous convalescence. He felt he could pronounce his recovery as complete and started back to work.

His first day downtown was miserable. He suddenly realized something was seriously wrong with his *back*. More specifically the hundreds of small ligaments of his back between the shoulder blades would seem to bunch up in an agonizing spasm of pain, very much like a thousand individual "toothaches" of the back.

When he went home the pain would disappear. He decided he would try to do some artwork at home. But every time he sat up to do a job of painting or drawing, the pain would return.

New, Expensive Pills

His physician ordered X rays and some expensive new pills, declaring the ailment "simple arthritis." The doctor had no time to try to explain why the pains came only on an entry into the downtown area or when the subject set up his drawing board to do artwork at home.

The failure of the pills, the lack of compassion of the physician, and principally the pain, oddly occurring only under two specific circumstances, caused the man to try Perfect Living. A friend advised him to say "Change" when going downtown or approaching his drawing board at home—to say "Change" without thinking of the meaning of the word, but to so believe in its *efficacy for banishing pain,* that he *wanted* pain to go, that he wanted the bigger side of himself to take command of his whole person and straighten out an ailment too odd for a doctor to bother with.

The switchword did bring instant relief, though not an instant cure. Today when going downtown or setting up for a drawing session at home, he still gets the ominous pain warnings from the hundreds of little ligaments in his back. But the switch dispels them for hours at a time and allows the artist to proceed with his life and his work in a normal fashion without submitting to a fate of acknowledged "arthritic" misery.

Comment:

The painful trouble may not have been caused by arthritis but more likely by the man's own anti-conscious seeking to exact a price in continuous pain for his recovery from a more serious sickness.

CASE:
He Took Up Tennis At Forty

This is a case of a *thing* serving as a switch instead of a *word*. A man just passed forty was urged by a friend to take up tennis, a game he had never played in his youth. This man, a great competitor and a firm believer in his own ability, took up the game and doubtless played it far more decisively and successfully than a "newcomer" of forty should.

In a few months, however, he found himself beginning to walk with an affectation of one of his hips, and frequently on sudden moves would feel swift, sharp surges of pain in his right hip joint.

X rays definitely showed an advanced arthritic condition at this point, and the man was advised to stop his vigorous tennis, which he did. But as in nearly all cases of an advanced arthritis, he was advised to settle down to live with his ailment and take necessary pills for pain.

Together in Fast Rhythm

This gentleman was not the kind of a quitter to do just that. A smattering knowledge of Perfect Living suggested that he repeat the word "Together" in this rhythm:

> Together, together, together, together!
> Together, together, together!
> Together, together, together, together!
> Together, together, together!
> Together, together, together, together,
> Together, together, together;
> Together, together, together, together,
> Together, together, together!

He said the same word twenty-eight times in a swinging rhythm and so fast it would be almost impossible to think of the meaning of each word separately.

This inspired chant worked what our friend, an indomitable man of spirit, did not hesitate to call a "miracle." Not only did his rapidly recited litany give him immediate relief from his pain, more importantly it started him on a concentrated project of studying his own "arthritis" with far greater care and sympathy than any doctor could give him.

Study proved his greatest hip pains came while in bed attempting to sleep. He began to experiment with new positions for his body in its prone, supine, and side positions. Habit tried to tempt him to stick with his lifelong position but *want* kept him changing, observing, and reporting to himself.

"Pillow" Was the Switch

What he was doing, he now realizes, was *trying to find the proper switch to cure his arthritis*. Spiritized and energized in his study and experiments by the TOGETHER CHANT OF TWENTY-EIGHT, he discovered the switch in a couple of weeks. It was a thing (not a word), and the thing was *pillow*.

It was a separate, extra pillow, which he started to hug as he set himself for sleep and which allowed his body to assume a shape and position where his hip joint could not grind against itself. In a month he was walking at his regular gait without trace of a limp.

Though this case happened over eight years ago, he has had absolutely no recurrence of the pain or hip crippling. And he declines to have any X rays to determine the cure medically, for he is completely satisfied with the switch to stave off any recurrence —"Pillow."

Experiment in Chanting

A certain degree of skepticism is bound to follow the reading of the above case history. It would be well for the reader at this point to prove something to himself.

The Together Chant of Twenty-Eight is a soul-conditioner. If you are bothered by nervousness, frustration, despair, fear or any of the multitude of negative ailments that assail people in middle age or older, please try this experiment.

If you are younger, relaxed, carefree to the point of lacking only one thing you would like to have (money), please try the same experiment.

Twenty-Eight Fast Chants

Take the word TOGETHER, and chant it to yourself twenty-eight times just as fast as you can say it, too fast to dwell even for a moment on the meaning of the word. You will note a great difficulty, practically an inability, to complete even two of the eight lines of the chant, without stopping to sigh or breathe out in relief.

Try as you may to stop yourself from sighing or breathing out, you will find it almost impossible, provided you are reciting the twenty-eight identical words fast enough.

And the sigh feels fine. The recitation has an instantaneous therapy. You feel good. You know you have done something worthwhile, *something which worked.* If you are the young, non-nervous, relaxed and healthy animal, the chant may not bring you one relief-charged sigh after another, but say it fast enough, and it will undoubtedly start you doing something practical for yourself, something extremely useful and thereby pleasing.

CASE:
The Slowdown of the Fast Pulse

Subject was in hospital bed when visited by a Perfect Living student Patient explained his trouble to his friend. He was afflicted with an abnormally high pulse rate; his heart, he said, was beating something like one hundred and twenty times a minute instead of the normal of approximately seventy beats. It was a trouble that had attended the patient for years—a high pulse rate overworking his heart and threatening him with heart failure.

"How many times a day does the nurse read your pulse?" asked the visitor. "Several times, and much too often," said the patient, "and she's due here any minute."

He was told a little about the theory of Perfect Living very quietly and invited to participate in a harmless experiment. "I'll stick around 'til the nurse shows," said his conspiring friend, "and when she starts to read your pulse don't do anything for ten seconds and then suddenly say 'slow.' Address the word to yourself in a mild, believing attitude much the same as shoving a slice of bread into an electric toaster."

The stunt was agreed on. The nurse soon appeared. The visitor said nothing. The nurse, feeling the patient's pulse with a professional look of concern, suddenly jumped to alertness. The man's heartbeat of a hundred and twenty suddenly dropped to seventy—no notice, no warning, no explanation. The nurse's face and manner showing sudden astonishment, she said aloud, "Guess I'll have to start over." By this time the patient's heartbeat had resumed its abnormal super-rate and the nurse smiled in renewed assurance, when suddenly again the patient was signaled by his visiting friend to say a silent "Slow" and the abrupt pulse slow-down followed.

Nurse Was Shaken Up

The nurse was forced to leave the room after making a note on her chart which some doctor later would disbelieve. She was shaken up. Visitor swore patient to secrecy, meanwhile stressing that the switchword certainly worked under the harsh test of a third party's supervision, and might help the patient further in his illness. On subsequent visits from nurses he had a lot of fun and ultimately became the mystification of the whole hospital staff, nurses and doctors alike.

Continuous repetitions of the switchword "Slow," uttered automatically and without meaning, restored his heartbeat to near normal when all the modern medicines had failed.

Switch for a Long Journey

One of the toughest of today's middleweight prizefighters is at his best when going in a fifteen-round championship bout. Every minute of every round, especially the early rounds, he switches on his stamina machine with the switchword "Fifteen." This switch activates the automatic experience machine which correctly paces the fighter so that he does not run out of gas in the early rounds.

Much the same kind of pacing happens when the experienced motorist is making a long automobile trip, say two hundred miles. He never reminds himself about the complete distance, but rather concentrates on getting HALFWAY there, in this case one hundred miles. His switch is "Halfway."

Half of the first halfway is fifty and that's not too hard to make without getting tired. Then fifty more is all that is necessary for the first full halfway. The rest of the journey can be broken into halfway points, not rationally or intentionally, but rather automatically with the switchword "Halfway" or "Half."

Thus any job or any task ordinarily described as long can be met with the simple switchword "Halfway." Of course if the work or project is particularly distasteful or even hateful, the switchword most often used is "Adjust." "Adjust" switches on more psychological endurance; "Half" or "Halfway" activates the machine which delivers more physical endurance.

Letter From Student:
He Creates Better While in Motion

"I agree with you that the switchword 'On' is a marvelous instrument for helping one secure quick transportation when none is in sight. I would also like you to know that I have heard you suggest the same word 'On' as a switch to produce instant creativity.

"In several experiments I have proved this out, especially when I am searching for new ideas or creative solutions of problems while riding in any vehicle such as a car, a cab, a train, or an airplane. Ideas seem to come by the dozen when I find myself in a moving conveyance and the switch is used with the clean-cut objective of creating a new idea.

"I have suggested the experiment to friends and they have reported it successful in several instances."

The Man
Whose Gray Hair Turned Dark

A group of "old grads" were discussing Perfect Living at an alumni banquet, and one experimenter, a man over 60 with hair now nearly white, raised the question of whether Perfect Living might carry a cure for baldness or perhaps a means of bringing back color to his gray hair. The subject lent itself to much humor, but one old grad, Frank J., decided to give it a try. He accepted the switchword "Back" as the activating switch to turn on the experience machine for restoring hair color.

He spent days in examining old photos of himself taken before he became gray; then further days on the thought of getting his hair back to its original color. It should be noted here that not all objectives are equally solvable in terms of necessary time. Perfect Living theory declares nothing is impossible if all forces are properly applied, but difficult objectives take more time than simple ones.

One Month to Get Results

It took our "old grad" about a month to get someplace. Results came from a dandruff preparation he stumbled on in hi intensive search for youthful hair color. The dandruff cure actually darkened his hair by several shades, removed the sickly yellow-gray cast it had held for years, and returned him to a young man's appearance. At a subsequent meeting with former classmen, when asked how he did it, his joking answer was "mental concentration."

To those who insisted on knowing exactly what he had done he told the full story right down to the name of the dandruff-removing agent. On this truthful revelation of his changed appearance, our friend, Frank, was greeted with loud guffaws of disbelief and the general remark: "Ole Frank always was a genius at confusing people."

CASE:
The Wallet That Worked Like a Relic

At the time this event happened, the author had been engaged for an extensive period in a study of psychokinesis, a common word for which might be "Stuff" or "Something on the ball."

This "Something on the ball" is the extra stuff a baseball pitcher has over and above mere speed, curves, or control, the extra and preternatural substance by which he makes the ball break physical laws and behave in an unexplainable way.

The Wallet Had "Something On The Ball"

The author, in his investigations of Perfect Living, was seeking out certain things as switches, things which might be even more effective than wordswitches. His findings in psychokinetics were closely related. At that time a great aunt, aged eighty-four, was suddenly taken to the hospital with an advanced case of dropsy, and after two weeks of treatment the doctors gave her up, conceding her one month to live.

The author then came up with this theory on "stuff" that an

object made with great craftsmanship by an acknowledged craftsman might work on the sick lady in much the same way that religious relics had healed others in the past.

He had a new hand-made wallet, the product of a famous bookbinder; the wallet had been made according to the rules for working in fine leather handed down by several centuries of artisans.

He brought the wallet to the sickbed of his aunt, merely saying: "Keep this in your bed, rub it every once in a while, put it under your pillow when you sleep."

In two days the doctors urged the old lady be taken home to die—which she did not. At home still handling and believing in the leather wallet, she began to improve. We then decided to change from the doctor who had given her up, sought out a new doctor (all of us perhaps still under the spell of the miraculous wallet), and it just happened that the new doctor diagnosed the case as a type of dropsy easily controllable with a brand-new drug! The lady whose life was saved by the wallet-switch lived to be ninety-two before dying of other causes.

The Craftsman's Explanation

The craftsman who made the wallet was told the story. I insisted he had put some of his own *soul* into the object, which worked the miracle. He insisted that perhaps he was only the instrument of the work of his craftsman-predecessors, who had put their many combined souls into the rules by which such objects had been made for centuries.

Regardless of whether the case belonged in Perfect Living or preternatural realm, we knew the old lady's faith contributed most to working the cure. When you believe in the switch and the experience machine behind it, the desired result is usually realized.

CASE:
Her Intense Want Infected Her Husband

The housewife had lost her coin purse. "Lost" it in the sense of not being able to find it. It contained a little money but that did not bother her so much; it was the loss of her identification, her driver's license, her house keys, and other essentials that concerned her.

For a day she searched the house up and down, her husband not paying too much attention to her distress, though marveling at the intensity of her want. The want continued to build up. All the housewife could do was associate the coin purse with some laundry she had sent out. On the second day, the husband heard her calling the laundry to search through the contents of the laundry bag. He watched her, normally a sedate and calm woman, running around the house like a chicken with its head chopped off.

Found Among the Clothespins

Such intense want is infectious, much the same as the want of some child for a certain Christmas gift. He became infected—but instead of rushing around wildly, the husband calmly said "Reach" and allowed his body and mind to go automatic.

"Where do you keep your clothespins?" he asked his wife. "Clothespins, clothespins!" she exclaimed as if in a daze and rushed downstairs to the basement. There in the small bag in which she kept her clothespins was the lost coin purse.

Want Alone Could Have Done It

The housewife's want was so overpowering that want alone might have ultimately found her coin purse for her. The husband's want, though secondhand, was a definite want just the same, and a requisite to a Perfect Living action. His use of the switchboard "Reach" made the want pay off a little sooner.

Experiment in Dispensing
With Your Clock or Watch

Can you tell the time of day at any given moment without consulting a clock or watch? This is an experiment at reading yourself out loud. Truly, everyone has a feeling that he always should know the time. And you actually *do know the time right down to a minute,* only you lack the ability to announce the correct time out loud.

Since the real you, the total you, does know the time because it has been *experienced* and your time experience machine holds the right time just as truly as a mechanical clock, to be successful at time-reading you must get together with yourself. Submit to the bigger part of yourself, the buried invisible you, and believe. Believing, now say "Reach," the switchword for finding something lost or solving a problem. Let yourself go. Refuse to guess. Read yourself and firmly believe in the reading.

Right now, without consulting your watch, tell us: What time is it? Check later to see how close you come. This is a very good practice for achieving the benefits of reading yourself out loud (getting closer to yourself), and continued practice will deliver phenomenal ability for producing Self-Togetherness.

Experiment in "Duplicate" Handwriting

As noted previously, a living person other than yourself often becomes a switch for delivering the feedback experience that brings Perfect Living.

Think of a person who is always extraordinarily pleasant, say his or her name, then firmly *want* to be pleasant, and immediate pleasantness will come to you. You can actually feel these results being delivered under your eyes.

When you are writing a letter to a close relative such as a sister, brother or parent, notice how your own handwriting begins to resemble the handwriting of the one to whom you are sending the letter.

This strange result might be listed as a form of imitation, suggestion, or autosuggestion, and as adherents of Perfect Living we have no quarrel with any art or science which taps out the almost infinite experience we hold inside ourselves.

Next time you are writing to a loved one, make the test a Perfect Living test, tell yourself you want to write in the hand of the person who will get the letter. Speak his or her name silently as a switch. You will be astonished at the result.

21

THE
MAGIC POWER
OF WANTING

An ASTONISHING NUMBER OF SUCCESSES HAVE BEEN SCORED in the use of the switchword "Change" to relieve or remove any object which has gotten into the human eye. It has been already noted that in close to a hundred cases there has not been a single failure.

If victims forget or ignore the device or use some other wrong attempt they may fail, but never when they submit to personal automation, saying "Change." A janitor reports sixteen successes, a letter carrier eight, a switchman twenty-one, and so on.

Theory of the Pain-Producing WANT

An overpowering urge to get rid of an ailment that has become completely obnoxious forces the sufferer to find a way out of his trouble. Suffused with real want, his objective has become clear, the many sides of his personality have at last reached an agreement, and with both surface and subsurface togetherness, his resources for banishing the trouble are unlimited.

No Time to Pick a Fight

So it is with something in the eye. Psychopathically one might in his subconscious actually welcome slowly failing eyesight, or an eye affection such as a cataract or a weakening muscle. These things are slow-forming and sneak in without conscious notice. But an unwanted object suddenly getting into the eye is a FAST trouble. The subconscious has to react to the pain so fast that it has not any time for picking a fight with the conscious or seeking sly revenge. It wants the object out! The conscious side wants the same thing. Instant agreement ensues between the feeling and thinking souls.

If in the throes of this situation the individual submits at once to Perfect Living and allows himself to become an automaton obeying its laws, he never tries to dig the object out or fight it out. Quickly and carefully he may decide to close the lids; to touch the eye gently; to keep the lids closed and then to open them at a given moment; to lift the lid; to keep the eye closed for a protracted time; to sense when the object has floated onto a lid and then to open the eye and examine it visually; or to follow any of a hundred other maneuvers.

"Stretch"

A survey was made among a group of experimenters in Perfect Living. These experimenters had been instructed and drilled in use of the switchword "Stretch" to prolong a period of fine feeling, once the fine feeling had entered the person by accidental or natural means.

Seventy percent of the answers indicated the experimenters

were convinced that "Stretch" actually did prolong the feeling of
high invulnerability which is the outstanding mark of the Perfect
Living state. Thirty percent confessed that though "Stretch"
seemed to be an immediate booster, it could not protect them
from the onslaughts of negative things in life, from fear, worry,
pain; setbacks caused by other people. The majority of this thirty
percent reported that when they noted a feeling of disunion or
apartness was threatening, they resorted to other devices for
dispelling fear, worry, irritation, with a fair measure of success.

This is the correct attitude. Until Perfect Living had been
completely understood and comprehensively mastered, only what
may be called "singular" instances of its successful workings can
be reported. Eventually Perfect Living should deliver for us the
Perfect Person, and not just in a single case, but by the legion.

Of the seventy percent who reported definite success with the
switchword "Stretch" for the prolongment of good feeling, comments were very significant.

He Bowled 747

"I found myself in a hot streak while bowling. It seemed like
I couldn't do anything wrong and I felt like a million dollars. As
the pins kept falling I suddenly realized I was in a grand state of
Self-Togetherness. But knowing that bowling is a game of ups
and downs, I began to chant to myself: 'Together—stretch,' 'Together—stretch.' I finished with a three game series of 747! My
regular bowling average is 140, and of course, I had never come
anywhere near this figure in all my days."

Author Comments on a Resolution

"I have found the switch 'Stretch' very effective at prolonging
the strength of a resolution, such as to cut down on food, drink, or
smoking. I clearly re-state the resolution, then say 'Stretch.' It
does marvels at reinforcing my will power to abstain."

Comment by author: What subject is doing here is recalling and dwelling on the Self-Togetherness that was engendered in the first place by the resolution (objective); its enactment in the early stage (want); its reinforcement by continuing abstinence ("will power") and the subsequent seeing eye-to-eye of all sides of the person, and thus the securing of the state of no inner conflict.

The author has not the slightest doubt that the switchword "Stretch" will work in cases where temporary Self-Togetherness has been achieved. Individual case histories justify this belief. This prolonging of the happy state may continue for hours with the help of "Stretch" if no major negative setbacks ensue for the individual. But regardless of the number of new influences which seek to steal away his Togetherness state, that state will be prolonged for a definite period in spite of negative attacks whether from without or within.

Mysterious Cases

Want is often allied with need, and belief with pride. When your automobile has just been polished and given a brand-new appearance, the motor (which has not been touched) not only seems to run better, but actually does perform better. Your pride in the car's brilliant appearance draws from your hands and arms and feet a kind of sympathetic coordination which definitely invites the best performance from the engine.

The Elevator Stopped on Her Wish

A stenographer taking a down elevator from the 41st floor wanted to get off at 12, and temporarily forgot that she also had an errand on 31 on the way down. Just before 31 our steno remembered 31 and ejaculated her lapse of memory to the other passengers in the elevator. But the elevator stopped at 31 anyhow.

Now we do not claim that buried intention or sudden want did the trick here, and probably the best explanation was that some one did press the button outside 31 and then was called away.

But dozens of cases of extrasensory communication have been reported in connection with electric current. It seems that you often think of someone who has not seen you in ages and then next moment he calls you on the telephone. You are looking at television and you begin to predict some singular action will immediately happen and it does.

Private Telepathic Machines?

Undoubtedly the participants in the extraordinary acts or predictions have unknowingly switched on their private telepathic machines and unconsciously worked out the feats with no system being used. All these cases, however, can be utilized by further conscious analysis and often a new working switch is discovered.

Undoubtedly, the delayed action in the scores of cases reporting the finding of lost articles a day or two after the switchword "Reach" was invoked may be explained by the subject having silently ticked off the switch "Stretch."

In such instances of delayed action, followers report that on finding the lost article (a day or two or even a month later) they cannot stop themselves from giving Perfect Living full credit for the success, though it was delayed.

Judy Garland

This great spirited singer and actress had suffered a serious breakdown and for a long time was out of the public eye. But her comeback was sensational. She freely gives credit to the musical instruments that were definitely associated with her return to prominence and popularity, the timpani. Now anytime she feels set back by any little disappointment, she says to herself: "Timpani" and through personal automation pulls herself out of the blues instantly.

We have had reports of many cases of individuals who, in testing Perfect Living have drawn on personal history, consciously and with rational justification, for switches that worked. In fact most switches based on past events that represented glory or good fortune are used frequently by individuals, all unconscious of the intricacies of personal automation.

Cases of Act, Fact, Symbol

Often an act or a fact or a symbol may turn out to be the switch that sets off an automatic chain of events.

Power in a Mental Photograph

In hundreds of cases the mental photograph of an exact objective, constantly held before the inward eye, has acted as a continuous switch for automatically inducing the person to do all the efficient and strategic things necessary for him to reach a goal.

Flag an inspiration

The flag of any nation, clean, large and prominently displayed, not only causes citizens to think patriotically, but often causes many special automatic acts of patriotism that the doers hardly realize they are doing.

Work Up a Sweat Before the Speech

Many actions become switches, all unconscious, for the attainment of conscious goals. Public speakers have long ago learned the trick of doing some hard, even sweaty, physical work as the time for an important speech approaches. The aim here is to dispel FEAR. The ordinary word-switch would be "Bluff!" But orators who have investigated many facets of Perfect Living report that physical action, like shoveling snow, walking fast, moving chairs or tables or other weighty objects, just before a speech, adds to the power of "Bluff," and helps to rid the personality of every last trace of fear.

Reports on "Be" for Form

Many reports, some sensational, have been received concerning the use of the switchword "Be" as a device for switching on the experience machines that deliver the thing athletes and others call "form" which in turn delivers phenomenal scores.

One softball player, fifty-five years old, playing in a picnic game, used "Be" as a switch for recalling the form he had thirty years before and got eleven hits in a row. Various old-timers in football and baseball, when called upon to play in games their age should forbid, have used the switch to deliver great performances against younger rivals.

Prizefighters, both amateur and professional, have reported calling on the switch when the tide was going against them, putting them behind on points; while the switchword "Be," when invoked, turned the tide in their favor. Artists and writers also have noted signal success.

Avoid "Imperfect Living"

Commentary: It may at first be difficult to explain why individuals who produce outstanding and visible results with the switches seldom remember to use them in *all* cases involving new objectives.

We are all prone to slip back into old habits of thinking, feeling, and acting which are the reasons for IMPERFECT LIVING.

Only after enough experience in the new system, enough personal proof of its efficacy, and acceptance by the majority of men, their teachers, exemplars, and influencers, will we *automatically* and *instinctively* slip into the habit of using Perfect Living on all our problems, distresses, and objectives. It seems that any time a "near-miracle" is performed (some superior-to-natural accomplishment), we are all willing to let it go at that. We fail to resume any attempts to nail down the principles and requirements for repeating the act.

He Won the Drill Competition With a Stone in His Shoe

Two soldiers drilling in boot training were marching side by side. One muttered to his friend (a Perfect Living student), "I just got a stone in my shoe and I'm limping through this drill." The friend knew his pal was trying for a good mark since he wanted to get into officers' training school. "Say 'Change'," he urged. " 'Change!' Are you nutty?" was the astonished whisper. "No, say it to yourself or whisper it out loud to me and tell yourself you want to get that object out of your shoe while still drilling."

The soldier did as advised and the pain ceased at once. The soldier stopped limping and went on to win first prize as the best-drilled man in the entire regiment.

One Lost Ball Gets Him Four

On a bad hole in a golf game, a participant lost his golf ball. Searching, he said "Reach" and immediately found, not only his own ball, but three other lost balls!

"Care" Is a Fine Switchword for Sensational Feats of Memory

The human brain, in unusual cases, often produces feats that could shame the electronic brain by comparison.

In the annals of the British Society for Psychical Research there is related the case of a domestic in a wealthy home displaying an amazing memory. The maid was sick in bed with a high fever when she suddenly began to recite page after page of *Latin* —a language she knew nothing about. For hours at a time, rhythmically and with fine pronunciation, she would recite Virgil. She had never even heard of Virgil and never read a line of his Latin verse. In fact, when the fever subsided she did not know what she had done.

Research, however, showed that this girl had worked a few years before in the home of a college professor. This professor, in his study, would often read long passages of Virgil aloud. The maid working nearby often overheard many of these readings. But, of course, she never wanted to memorize them.

The words, however, were engraved somewhere in her brain and high fever brought them forward in her subconscious to be announced out loud. The fever automatically switched on a memory mechanism that was normally unconscious.

He Passed His Exam Too Fast

A college student reports he used the word "Reach" to discover the elements in a chemical solution being given to students in his class in analytical chemistry. Each student had his own bottle and was instructed to find out the five different chemicals in it. The previous semester's work was to be employed in finding the answer. The test ordinarily took more than an hour of comprehensive experiment. But this student simply looked at his bottle, said "Reach," immediately wrote down the names of five different elements, and in a matter of minutes turned in his report.

Since his answers were not only correct, but also written down in the very same order in which the professor had written the contents in his own secret book, the student was immediately challenged and accused of cheating. "No one could get the answers that fast without stealing them from my book," said the chemistry professor.

Though the student protested his honesty and furthermore tried to explain his legitimate right to use the science of Perfect Living whenever he wanted to, his mark was withheld. He was told he must meet the professor in person, privately, a week later and explain in detail exactly where those answers came from.

He Memorized 15,000 Words in One Day

Student, undismayed, again fell back on Perfect Living—this time the switch "Care," for *remembering.*

Saying "Care" occasionally, he leafed through the mimeographed lessons of the past five months, some 15,000 words—and found he was able to recite almost all the material by heart. Demanding an early interview, he faced his challenger and beginning at Lesson One proceeded slowly and deliberately, to recite the lesson *word for word.* Forty-five minutes passed and he was just in the middle of Lesson Two, when the listening professor threw up his hands, pleaded guilty of a wrong accusation and humbly apologized to the student.

This time, our smiling young friend passed with the highest possible chemistry mark, did not attempt to explain his "explanation" which was a feat in automatic memorization and nothing more.

For Fingernail Biters

Thousands of strong, sane and "normal" adults bite their fingernails. These people are really "eating themselves up." Many are handsome women who chew their nails down to the bone and keep them thus chewed all through life. If it were well-nigh impossible to find one fingernail chewer in a large city, the strange habit would be called sensational and lengthy treatises would appear in medical journals. But there is nothing rare or notable about fingernail chewers—there are too many of them. Every one of them is engaging in a continuous act of bad living just as egregious as that of the man who was trying to break his own instep in his sleep.

The "incurable insomniac" is the same man who uses a hundred tricks to keep himself awake, all the while bemoaning the fact that he cannot sleep.

The same switch "Off" has worked for both insomniac and fingernail chewer. But it must be noted that where the trouble is really awful, and definitely abnormal, all the essential attributes of Perfect Living must be intensively present to hope for a quick cure.

Broke Habits by Extraordinary Means

One fingernail chewer, introduced to the principles of Perfect Living, broke himself of the habit by adopting a homemade slogan: *"Together to Stay—Together for Good."* He repeated this slogan as he would a religious aspiration, endlessly, day and night. He asserts that it brought him into the proper "Together" mood, in which state he found the switch "Off" powerful enough to block him automatically when he was unconsciously tempted to chew his nails.

"ALWAYS A FIRST TIME"

The old saying, "There's always a first time," explains many a case of a wrong objective being subconsciously implanted in the individual.

You may never have had a fire in your house, but if you think too often of a fire happening, the buried subconscious contrives to help you see the unwanted objective reached. Unless you say "Cancel" when the thought of a fire, or a burglary, or an arrest, or a shooting, or some other frightful event comes into your mind, you may eventually experience a catastrophe your conscious mind could never want.

"Cancel" is a fine working switch for staving off the unwanted "first time."

Case of the Wandering Topcoat

A few years ago, the author of this book lost his new topcoat one evening in a New York restaurant and next morning the coat walked into the author's office in Chicago on another man's back, with the stranger thinking he was wearing his own coat, though it was about five sizes too large for him.

The case was a magical illustration of the power of the switch-word "Reach" when one seeks to find a lost article, and inserts into the project a super-supply of WANT.

I had dined alone in a restaurant near Grand Central Station, and checked my coat in its checkroom.

But my check failed to deliver it, the checkgirl was unable to find it, and the manager courteously implored me to wait till the current round of diners had changed and claimed their coats, for then my coat was sure to turn up.

Coat Was Gone

But after two hours of waiting, my coat did not appear, and I began to raise a rumpus. All the manager could do was find an old worn gabardine topcoat that had not been claimed that evening.

We went through the coat, seeking identification. Though we were in New York, the coat had a Chicago label inside and a heavy bunch of keys, apparently home, office, and car keys. It seemed clear at this point that the owner of that coat had taken it by mistake, for otherwise the keys would not have been left behind. I was assured that after I had waited a little longer, the owner would discover his mistake and bring back my lost coat.

Waited and Waited

I waited and waited, then would leave for ten minutes and come back. On each return another complete search of the un-claimed coat would ensue.

It is amazing how many clues one can find where there are so few clues. We studied the keys, the label in the coat, the contents, two toothpicks, a rubber band and a scrap of old yellow paper with an unreadable note scribbled on it. Near midnight a new checkgirl found a name written on the old yellow paper, a name which was not that of the coat owner clearly, just a name.

A Series of Long Distance Calls.

I then began a series of long distance phone calls, finally got this man on a telephone in a small town in Illinois and from this conversation proceeded to guess at a connection, farfetched, which involved the name of a man from Chicago, who spent half his time in the East and who happened to be the landlord from whom I rented office space in Chicago.

No one knew where he stayed in the East, but by passion, drive, bulldog *want,* I located the man's wife in another small town, this time in Jersey, found he and she had eaten dinner that night in that same restaurant, had left with a topcoat on his arm and taken the train back to Chicago.

Located at Last

I had located the coat, and going back to my hotel fell into an exhausted sleep. Next morning I called my partner in Chicago just as the landlord was passing by the door of our office and my partner stopped him to say: "Mr. X, you are wearing M's coat." (Sleeves were at least five inches too long.)

He put his hands in the pockets and from one pocket drew two hotel keys. My New York key was one; his Chicago key (he had just registered that morning) was the other.

One key was 1915, the other 1916, from two different hotels in two different cities. After the episode, which had several other startling "coincidences," I computed the number of chances of it happening again as one in Six Septendecillion, Seven Hundred and Fifty Sexdecillion, with all circumstances the same.

But I had beaten the percentage against me and recovered my coat by *wanting* it and continuing to invoke Perfect Living with the switch "Reach."

How Three People Helped Themselves

Learned to Walk Like a Cat

A coronary patient was forced to take large dosages of anti-coagulant medicine, which thins the blood and subjects the user to easy bruising or bleeding.

At first he noticed himself bumping into the furniture more often than he used to do, causing black and blue marks all over his body. His hands, too, would show disfiguring marks for every little bump and scratch. He was given the switch "Adjust," and he used the word generously, especially when approaching any physical thing in his path. Now his friends tell him he walks as gracefully as a cat, and his body and hands have lost the bruise marks.

Couldn't Live Without TV

Young Fred, just out of high school, was a TV fan, and sat glued to his set all day and evening. His parents planned to send him out of town to a small college, where there definitely was no television.

"But I can't live without television," protested Fred. As he left for college, his father gave him a tip. "Every time you think about how much you miss TV," he advised, "simply say: 'Adjust' and tell yourself you WANT to get along without it because you HAVE to."

On his first vacation home, Fred never went near the TV set. Asked to explain, he remarked: "I thought I couldn't live without it, but now I find I have no desire to watch television."

Two Towels Cured Him

A young man, in the home building business, one morning came down with a strange ailment. Suddenly he noticed his body was covered with round red spots each about the size of a half dollar. Hurriedly he visited his doctor, only to be told: "Frankly I don't know what this is. You'll have to give me a few days to get in touch with a specialist who may have heard of something like this."

But the young man, more frightened by the sight of the spots than distressed by any pain or discomfort, asked an investigator in Perfect Living if he could do anything. He was told: "Just say 'Change' and let yourself go automatic." The builder studied himself after saying the switchword before his next shower, found that he had been using too small a towel to dry himself. Again he said "Change" and reached for two larger bath towels.

One towel was not enough to dry his big body, and the second towel removed all moisture and bits of building dust which had evidently imbedded in his skin to produce some kind of an allergy. In two days, the spots, the size of a half dollar, were all gone while his befuddled doctor was still trying to find some specialist who had heard of half-dollar spots all over the body.

How Three People Fall Asleep

Getting to sleep is a real job for many. One office executive burdened with the details of the day which he inevitably takes to bed with him, received a quick briefing on the essentials of the use of switchwords. Then he proceeded to forget most of the instructions.

However, he remembered "Together" as a potent switch, and "Cancel" as a good switch for erasing bad mind pictures. So now all he says as he hits the bed is: "Together—Cancel," and he is asleep in a matter of minutes.

Switchword Combined With Audible Breathing

A stenographer had trouble getting to sleep. A friend advised her to listen to her own breathing and thus keep her mind off everything else. It worked for a while, then she began to fall back to her old habit of tossing and turning and staying awake.

A friend told her a little about the switches, and suggested she use the word "Off." But by accident she combined "Off," the switch, with audible breathing, the trick, and it made a grand combination. Now falling to sleep quickly is no problem. She simply says: "Off," and quietly listens to her breathing.

Breakfast at Night—in Bed

Another poor sleeper, a man in his fifties, knew about the device for thinking of tomorrow's breakfast while trying to fall asleep. You make a picture of the delicious bacon and eggs, you taste the eggs, the bacon, the salt, the soul-satisfying raisin toast, the hot strong coffee, you savor the tantalizing smells of the food —the great breakfast that awaits you eight hours hence. Try it. It works all by itself with a great many poor sleepers.

But our friend, knowing something of the switch system, went further in his efforts to get to sleep faster. He not only envisioned the complete and thrilling breakfast eight hours ahead, but stated his objective: "I want to complete these eight hours of sleep in one fell swoop right now." So considering the eight hours "in the bag" and breakfast now ready, he used the switchword: "Done," and slept through the night without awakening. And he reports he no longer has any trouble getting to sleep.

The Power of Want

It should also be remarked that pain is one of the greatest want-producers man owns. Few of us go through life with a constant toothache; pains chase us to the dentist for treatment or removal of the offender. You have heard it said of some individual whose ambition was violent, "He wanted the thing so bad he could taste it!" Such is the power of want that once it is present the individual has no doubts about his wanting, no need to try to engender further belief in the wanting or in his power to achieve the objective. Want takes over because, if it is real want, all parts of him want the very same thing in exactly the same way.

Each success in Perfect Living is the best answer to developing belief in Perfect Living. Doubt can easily assail you as you face a new objective; your belief may not be up to par. This is the time to recall your previous successes, especially the phenomenal and unquestionable successes. Such successes, though definitely sensational, tend to be regarded as so natural they can easily be forgotten. So remember them as they happen; better still keep a written log of successes and consult it any time you feel you need extra faith for a new project.

22

YOU
ARE NOT ALONE

Yes, THERE IS HOPE, HOPE FOR ALL OF US, THE HOPE THAT Perfect Living will someday be a universal reality and the doors of heaven-on-earth will open.

For the anti-conscious is NOT a soul in itself, but merely a bad phase of your great undersoul, sometimes known as the Second Soul. This same subconscious soul, most often found to be waging war on yourself while you yourself wage war on it, has another phase, gloriously and wondrously beneficent, which we will call the Pro-Conscious. All too rarely it comes into play. But it has displayed its friendly powers to all of us on occasion, demonstrating its ability to produce a feeling that can be called peace of heart or peace of mind. In past cases, the feeling did not last for very long, but it was so wonderful we can still remember it and through meditation, bring back part of its joy.

Ways to Develop and Expand
the Pro-Conscious

You may be in a hurry leaving the house when you get an inward warning that you are forgetting something. You may not be able immediately to remember what you have forgotten but definitely you know there is this detail to be handled. This is your pro-conscious silently but surely seeking to be of service. This is your sub-soul in its good phase of trying to assist your conscious mind.

Say a Silent "Thank You"

Honor it! Thank it! Be truly grateful to the point of whispering words of thanks to your inner self. Concede that your powers of conscious thinking have fallen down and are now being saved by the side of you that thinks without words.

Your second soul can smell without your knowing it. It can taste, hear, feel and see without your conscious mind being aware of the action.

Their Antennae Work for Them

One sensitive motorist reports that he has on a few occasions *felt* an impending accident before he ever saw the material for the accident; this feeling helped him to prevent it. "Somewhere inside me," he says, "are delicate antennae which feel the mass or another moving object, or a suddenly stopping vehicle, seconds before my eyes can announce the fact."

Another motorist was driving late at night toward a southern Florida city. The sky was very dark and suddenly a torrential rain descended on the countryside. The motorist was trying his best to make shelter at a nearby town when, in the midst of the downpour, an inner voice told him: "Stop the car right here, this very second!" Responding automatically, because he had previously flipped the switch for safety: "Guard," he stopped his car in the middle of the road, and ten feet in front of him saw a big cow standing motionless right in his path. "If I hadn't thrown that safety switch and responded immediately, either the cow or I or both of us would have been killed in another second," reported the traveler.

He Never Forgot How to Fall

An ex-football player, now aged seventy, who had not played for fifty years, tripped over an abutment in pitch-black darkness and felt himself falling to a level four feet below. He, too, in the split second before he crashed had the wit to say: "Guard." Though he was in poor physical condition, his automatic reflexes were properly activated in an instant and he managed to turn *a complete somersault*, to land on a hard cement walk on his hands and chest.

Only a few scratches, instead of a disastrous list of broken bones, resulted. His explanation: "When I played football half a century ago, I had learned how to fall. An old skill, not used for fifty years, came to the fore when I switched on my experience machine for self-protection. It surely saved me a wrecked body."

Can the Cowboy Smell the Water Before the Cattle?

Most dogs seems to know long before their masters when a storm is coming up. Many of them run under the bed. The cattle smell the distant water long before the cowboy, but if the cowboy only knew it, and trusted to his subconscious machinery, he could smell the water before the cattle!

We see men, deprived of one sense, develop another to an amazing degree. If the loss of one sense can bring about the high development of another, then it is obvious that all of our senses are subject to the same super-development without any of them being lost. These developments are not injections of new faculties; they are within our possession right now. William N. has lost his sense of smell, but he has brought his sense of hearing to the point where he can tell you if the pilot light on his gas stove is working or not working. Imagine, hearing a pilot light fifty feet away! If one man can do it when he has to, why are we not able to do it—or other such spectacular feats of sight, smell, taste and the like—when we are *not* forced to it by the loss of another faculty? The truth is, as modern scientists are now being forced to acknowledge, our senses, our brains, our intellect, and all our cognitive and sub-cognitive faculties, are only fractionally developed at present.

But Perfect Living holds the hope that such development need not have any limit. Taoism and the Chinese philosophers called the unlimited virtuosity of the human individual *SEN* and then refused to try to define SEN, because it was so immense all attempts to define it would only belittle it.

Establishing Personal Perspective

The first approach to Perfect Living lies in getting to know yourself through and through and in thus recognizing the relative importance of all of your parts one to the other.

In egomania we appear to insist that the total ego is the conscious person and we give little or no importance to the living abilities within us which are subconscious, unconscious, instinctive, surreal and otherwise nameless.

In experience, knowledge, skill, memory and in automatic responsiveness the conscious mind can never match the sub-soul with its quasi-infinite prowess. *The real ego is below the surface.* We notice that when we praise ourselves, that is, our *conscious side*, only discomfort and trouble ensues. When we praise others and thus deliberately ignore our own conscious feats, we are suffused with feelings of goodness and joy.

Self-sacrifice and unselfishness, viewed from the standpoint of sheer intelligence only, are not intelligent at all. Our conscious minds keep insisting, "Get all you can! Keep all you have!" But when you subordinate your conscious intelligence, it brings the conscious you closer to your real self and puts the total you into far better perspective with itself.

A New Slant on Self-Discipline

Self-discipline has long been considered a phase of man's conscious will demonstrating his mastery over his person, but now we know this is an inadequate concept. If self-discipline is to work it must include all the steps you take in using the powers and rights of your sub-nature.

The abstentions and sacrifices you make lower the importance of your conscious faculties and thus gain the good will and hearty cooperation of your sub-faculties.

A man with the "Talking Disease" (excessive and continuous verbosity) decides to remain silent for a full day or more. He then admits, "It is good for the soul to stop all this wild and foolish talking." It is more than that. The excessive talk was simple proof that his conscious mind had been running riot and trampling all over his sub-soul, attempting to grab credit for all of his so-called "wisdom." But when the conscious is K.O.'d, the whole person cheers. This sub-soul likes to see the garrulous, boastful conscious knocked out even for a day because proper perspective is then temporarily restored to the two souls of man.

Tips for Balancing the Psyche

If you talk too loud, try speaking quietly; try an occasional whisper. If you talk to others, talk about their pet subjects, their hobbies, their children, their jobs. Do not do it merely to be kind and sociable; do it deliberately to get your personal psyche into proper balance.

The intellect does not like physical work, so be sure to do some actual physical work—with your back, your hands—every day. The intellect is a snob in its natural dislike of physical work; hence when in a flash of self-inspiration it joins with the subconscious in such work, great mutual enjoyment results.

The very first law of all living things is: PRODUCE. Instinctively, if you cannot produce in the physical realm, you must try to sublimate the unceasing drive of your sub-soul and produce at higher levels, in a great speech, perhaps, or in a poem, a painting, a handmade object of art, a book, a design, or any accomplishment which has been achieved with great planning and thinking, and some degree of physical action thrown in to boot.

This is why a job superbly done so pleases the doer; he knows he is approaching Perfect Living. A few moments or hours of complete self-satisfaction then ensue. For a little while he is one with himself and at peace with the world.

Reading Yourself Out Loud

Perhaps the finest way in which you can honor your sub-soul and thus coax your pro-conscious machinery to deliver personal Togetherness is to engage in frequent attempts to read yourself out loud.

Ask the soul underneath questions like: "Just how do I feel right now?" "What exactly do I want?" "What is best for all of me?" "What am I doing wrong?"

Conventional truth, what society thinks or wants you to think on a given subject is readily at hand.

Logical truth, the product of your conscious reasoning, can be worked out too, if correct rational processes are used.

But *EMOTIONAL TRUTH,* so essential in any honoring of the sub-soul, generally remains a mystery.

The sub-soul remembers everything that ever happened to you or near you and there could never be time to report the vigintillion incidents and experiences involved in one single human life. If properly approached, however, the subconscious can transmit its rare and valuable feelings to the conscious mind. Poets and artists often reveal this gift for probing their inward selves and bringing to light emotional truth that startles the world of conventional thinking.

Their Stomachs Knew

Some years ago the dairy department of the University of Illinois had an ice cream "taste test." Five unknown brands of ice cream in unmarked cartons were submitted to a group of tasters. The tasters were asked to try all five and then announce their choices in order based on quality in general, butter-fat content, texture, taste, after-taste, and any other point that appealed to them.

Seldom did any participant name the ice creams in proper order, for mathematically there was only one chance in 3125 of *guessing* the right answers. The best in the five was an ordinary-looking ice cream, almost cheap in appearance. The second-best was really a ugly-looking yellow; and the tasters invariably let factors like appearance, sweetness, imaginary creaminess, determine their answers.

But the strange thing about the test was this: Always when the test was over, and the wrong answers tallied, the carton which had the least ice cream left in it was invariably the best, the next emptiest carton was the second-best and so on down the line with the carton that had the most ice cream left in it always being fifth.

The test showed conclusively that nearly everyone's tasting mechanism was perfect but that his conscious announcing mechanism was poor. The people who thought they knew ice cream could not read themselves out loud. Yet the very attempt to get at their true deep down feelings brought them a little closer to their true selves.

Sympathy From the Sub-Soul

When any individual decides on and accepts an objective that is truly good *for the whole being,* the subconscious soul exudes great evidence of friendship and cooperation. This is quite a rapid turnabout for Goethe's "second soul" which ordinarily wants to use its full powers to beat down the conscious. We have all heard of accomplishments by individuals who turned bad setbacks into brilliant stepping stones to success.

An amateur golfer had been invited to enter his first big tournament and on the morning in question took violently sick. After he had vomited for three hours and weakened himself to the point of exhaustion, he was urged by friends to withdraw from the tournament. Sick as a dog, he insisted on playing and proceeded to go through three rigorous games and win the tournament.

Here we see the animosity of the anti-conscious phase of the sub-soul for the pro-conscious phase of the same soul. The attacking soul went too far, hurt too much, made a mistake; then the pro-conscious phase went out to redeem the loss and delivered vast reserves of skill and strength because it hated to see a clean-cut objective ruined or abandoned.

Wrote 100,000 Words Standing Up

An author received a special assignment from his publisher to write a full-length book in a hurry. The assignment caught the writer in the middle of a prolonged attack of sacroiliac trouble. His bad back prevented him from sitting down at the typewriter, because if he sat down, he could not straighten up. Undaunted, the writer said "Adjust," automatically obeyed an inward suggestion, put his portable typewriter on a high dresser and in two months wrote a hundred thousand words standing up!

The pro-conscious, properly treated, is never phased by burdens or challenges; in fact, many individuals have so come to speaking terms with their "better halves," their inward selves, that they seem to love challenges and invite handicaps. This is the magic that lies in Initiative. Simply start a job, *though your conscious self be empty of material or energy for the job,* and very soon from within comes the heat and fuel for carrying your project through to completion.

Let Your Pro-Conscious Tell You What to Do

If you are sincere in developing your pro-conscious as an invaluable personal asset, you may reach the point where you can actually hear it speak wordlessly.

Fanny F. had been an inveterate coffee drinker but in late years had to admit her kidneys were going back on her. She had symptoms of excessive urination, dizziness, and fatigue, and decided to consult herself, using the switchword "Change." Listening carefully, she heard an inward voice say: "Give up coffee entirely!" That was almost as distasteful as being told she had to have a leg amputated, but Fanny tried it and has abstained from coffee for the past ten years. Now, at seventy-five, she says she never felt better in her whole life.

His Pro-Conscious Diagnosed His Trouble

A sensitive man heard this inward voice tell him: "Cut down on meats and spices." He was having aches in his joints, his arches, in parts of his body that had never ached before such as his neck, his thighs, his elbows. His doctor was treating him for very high blood pressure and getting no results. So our friend, newcomer to Perfect Living, cut down his intake of meat and hotly spiced food to a very minimum, not even knowing why. All he had done was say "Change," want to be rid of his troubles, and automatically followed the voice of his inward self.

His aches and pains disappeared in a week after he had demanded a uric acid test which showed he had the GOUT. The reduction of proteins in the diet, plus the intake of proper gout pills, were said to work the cure, but our friend, magnanimously, gave full credit instead to the pro-conscious phase of his own sub-surface self.

Attend That Wake

You hear that an acquaintance had died and a wake is in progress. The question is: Should you go or not? Your conscious mind begins to reason: "I did not know this fellow very well in life. I have other things to do. The funeral parlor is some distance away. If I do not go, no one will miss me." Your conscious concludes: "Better not go." Then, if you are listening and trying really to read yourself out loud, the voice within submits its side of the case. "Go! Go for no reason at all. Go—because the thought of going has entered your soul!"

So you submit and go. There is not much doing at the wake but as you leave you are elated because you have dragged your body to the spot and have done a good deed. You feel great and noble because your underself has helped you rise far above reason.

He Thought He Saw His Dead Cousin

A student of Perfect Living writes: "We are all too reluctant to recognize and acclaim the miraculous powers of our subter-ranean selves. How often these powers are made available and ignored.

"Last Sunday in church I found myself staring at the back of a man a few pews in front of me. From this view he seemed *identical* with a cousin of mine who had died a few months ago.

"Never in my life could I have been expected to describe or draw a picture of my cousin's head, neck, or shoulders as seen from such a rear angle. I kept staring and waiting for the man to turn his head ever so slightly. I would know whether his pivoting profile would coincide with my cousin's down to the smallest fraction of an inch. I began to marvel at my own perfect memory, my confidence in knowing the slightest variation in resemblance as soon as it would occur—only a tiny change in angle would be necessary and, when it finally happened, the difference was immense.

"But what I marveled at was the knowledge that I knew and remembered every last detail of my cousin's head, neck and shoulders. When one considers he knows just as much about the details of every mere acquaintance, he begins to appreciate the immensity of his own buried experience."

23

THE
GREAT JOY
OF PERFECT LIVING

Once YOU HAVE BECOME IMMERSED IN THE MAGIC OF Perfect Living, its experiments, its discoveries, you will begin to talk about it to your friends and close acquaintances. Something in your words, your voice, something more than EN-THUSIASM will get through to them and they will demand that you explain at once. In answer you will probably say: "Read the book." But you who are reading the book right now are entitled to a capsule review of what you have read.

First Proposition:

Man's Immediate Aim Is Permanent Self-Union

Man's first aim in life—first not in the sense of ultimate, but first in the sense of *immediate*—is to get together with himself, to stop the eternal war of his two adversary souls and become a single soul in a single body, a person in the complete and permanent state of Self-Togetherness.

If man so decides after achieving perfect and permanent self-union, he can then pursue any further aim in life such as God or pleasure, riches or fame, wisdom or love, power, health, or any of the other twelve basic objectives that have been his aims all through history. Once he has achieved Togetherness of Self, these other aims are comparatively simple to attain.

Second Proposition:

Perfect Living Is a State of Invulnerability

The state of self-union is not a state of uncontrolled ecstasy wild enthusiasm or insane fervor. Rather it is a definite heaven on earth best identified as a feeling of supreme invulnerability to harm or hurt or fear. It is guided by sane and prudent intellect with all negative feeling eliminated. Nothing but the natural state of man's original glory remains.

Third Proposition:

The Office Boy Everlastingly Fights With the President of the Corporation

As we view man in his present state of extensive distress and unhappiness, continuing day after day and only occasionally relieved by a sprinkle of joy and gladness, we must perforce surrender to the cosmic truth of these lines by the poet Goethe:

> There are two souls in my own breast
> and one is determined to beat down the other.

In this perspective, if each of us views himself as a big corporation, which he actually is in terms of personality, one soul is the office boy. This office boy is the rational side of the man, making all decisions, claiming all credit for success and placing all blame for failure on his other soul.

This other soul is the buried, invisible self of vast, unlimited experience. Unable to speak, it is, however, endowed by experience with an almost infinite ability to achieve specific desires and eliminate specific distresses.

This second soul of the man is the true president of the corporation. A thousand times every hour he is insulted by the office boy with inane suggestions, directions, lectures. Unable to fight back with words, this soul indulges in innumerable acts of revenge, interference, emotional upsets, fears and roadblocks, all of which take their toll by leaving the total man *a victim of imperfect living*.

In the resultant state we see man as he usually is, an individual of two warring souls, two enemy camps, a frightful example of APARTNESS.

Fourth Proposition:

You Must Believe in Your Underground Factory

To move towards Perfect Living, you must acknowledge the presence within yourself of a vast underground factory of the marvelous machines of your own experience. At present the machines are rusty and misaligned; but they are capable of being restored and brought back to unerring efficacy. Each machine in this factory is custom built either to eliminate a specific distress or achieve a specific desire.

Therefore, as a man of only one proper soul, you must view yourself, when on your own side and absolutely together with yourself, as being able to do almost anything within human limits. You must believe completely in yourself, in your own machinery, and in particular in the immense experience you have had in the realm of the unconscious, subconscious, and surreal—

in essence all the experience you have ever had which you cannot invoke by conscious means.

You must BELIEVE IN YOUR UNDERGROUND FACTORY. You must WANT to use it on every problem that cannot be solved by ordinary means.

Fifth Proposition:

You Can Control the Machines of Personal Automation and the Switches That Actuate Them

You can turn on the miraculous machines in your subterranean factory by flipping individual switches, which are generally switchwords; or sometimes pictures, symbols, or actions. Without conscious effort or aid, the machines of experience will go to work for you and in unseen, undetectable ways bring about the results you seek. The action is automatic. It is nothing more or less than personal automation. By a feedback process you have stored and restored all your experience of real life, of dream life, of imaginary life, of life over and above real life, of every category of emotion and unknowingly packed it away underground for future use.

Sixth Proposition:

"Together" Is the Master Switch for the Whole Underground Factory

After working your machines of experience long enough and well enough to believe in their efficiency, and after practicising all the rules of Perfect Living faithfully, you will no longer need to use individual switchwords to switch on individual machines.

You will need only to flip the master switch to the entire subterranean factory—the word TOGETHER—to achieve the perfect joy, the heaven on earth that is Perfect Living. From this state of perfection in self-organization you can then address yourself to any of the other Big Things you may want from life, knowing for certain that you will reach your goal.

SEEK YOUR FIRST GOAL FIRST

For all the ages of man he has only had a few real goals, and he mistakenly regarded them as first *goals*, when academically they were his choice of *ultimate* goals. But your greatest need and your very first goal should be to get together with yourself and to stay that way for every second of your life.

The Hints of Something Bigger

In all of man's studies, from the most abstruse mysticism of religion to the cold-blooded mystery of allergy, the presence of something bigger has always been suspected. Many of these mysteries, however familiar, have never been satisfactorily resolved, for example: phenomenal memory, genius, talent, hypnotism, dreams, the power of example, the power of suggestion, psychical phenomena, extrasensory perception, psychokinesis, nostalgia, self-confidence, fear, religious faith, religious miracles, instinct, intuition, passion, love, self-preservation, will power, surrealism, subliminal phenomena, the subconscious, the unconscious, and all the other workings of the human ego.

No Answer in the "Little Things"

Man's ineffectuality as a person is often revealed in his feeble attempts to find an answer to life in a wide variety of "little things." Some seek to prove that the ability to wear sports clothes relieves them from any further duty of thinking.

The pose is the thing. Women, trying to look young as they speed toward old age, will resort to the life of good clothes and dieting so that their two main topics of conversation are "What I wear" and "What I eat." Well-to-do men glory in the possession of a wardrobe of $300 custom-made suits and engage in prolonged flights of lah-dee-dah glee when examining new suitings and being measured for new suits.

Others convince themselves that the conventional business vocabulary is a good answer to life, so that, while saying nothing, they seem to be saying something. Great hordes of human beings plop down in front of television sets like vegetables which can see and hear.

Sports captivate the American man. Others seek answers in drinking, in politics, in work madness, in money madness, in leadership, in smutty story telling, in clowning, in becoming reading bums, in talking sprees, in gambling, or in sex indulgence. But none of these "escapes" ever release them from their prisons.

Apartness Vanishes When Submission Is Invoked

Submission by the Office Boy Conscious Mind and humble acknowledgment that the real President of the Personality is the great subsurface self is the first step in the direction of self-union.

Chastise the conscious soul by lowering your voice if it is loud, raising it if weak; stop talking for a whole day; abstain from bragging, fault-finding or complaining. Try to tell yourself the full truth about yourself—and you automatically invite your two warring sides to come together for an armistice.

This is the hour in which you must brazenly bluff yourself out of your fears and proclaim your own faith in yourself, in your almost infinite experience, in the push-button system for using your total experience, however acquired, however invisible.

The System at Work

When submission has succeeded in diminishing self-apartness and inducing a mood of inner togetherness, *this is the time to practice,* this is the time to test the switches on desires, distresses, specific objectives.

State your want and its objective clearly and rationally, silently or aloud or both, making your full self know the exact meaning of the objective.

Now *believe in your project,* in your individual role in this Perfect Living experiment, relying totally on the processes of personal automation without attempting to know what they are. Let your body act like a sleep walker or a subject in a semi-hypnotized state.

Now *throw the switch* that sets the individual machine into motion, *without thinking of the meaning of the switchword,* in much the same way as you would switch on the light, the vacuum cleaner, or a toaster in your own home.

Now, in a compliant mood of self-ductility, subjugate your reasoning processes to automatic reflexes.

Prompt Encouragement

Long ago the great Nietzsche observed:

> In every real man there is a child hidden—it wants to come out and play!

And just recently a lesser genius, Antonio Rocca, exclaimed:

> Love life and life will love you more. We will live to be 150 years. We are all in a dark room looking for a light switch—but everybody has the power to turn on the light!

Engage in enough attempts to use your subterranean machines and you will find prompt encouragement in the form of near miracles that cannot be explained by conventional means. Your personality will begin to inhale an immense tranquillity coming from the upsurge of the Togetherness within you. Prolong such periods of self-union with the switchwords "Stretch" and "Together."

Press on to realize your fulfillment as a Perfect Living person, one of unified power, free of pain and fear, capable of doing anything and enjoying everything—while living in your very own glorious, self-made paradise.